patch!

Cath Kidston

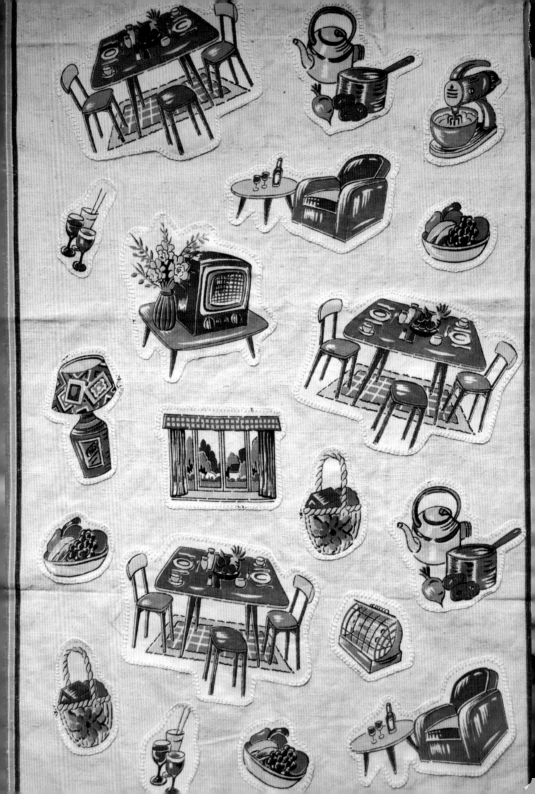

patch!

Cath Kidston

PHOTOGRAPHY BY PIA TRYDE

Quadrille
PUBLISHING

Introduction

Patch! is the fourth in my series of craft books, and this time I've taken the title very literally. As anyone who's visited my stores will recognise, all my designs are about reinterpreting the past and taking a more contemporary, colourful approach to tradition. Once I started to explore the fascinating theme of patching and pieced work, I became inspired by the possibilities. I discovered a huge wealth of historic ideas, and I've come up with over thirty projects which bring a new twist to these versatile techniques.

Patchwork evolved as a thrift craft in an era when new fabrics were scarce and expensive, so it is right on trend with today's ethos of sustainability and recycling. It simply involves sewing together pieces of fabric to create a larger design, a technique which encompasses everything from meticulously hand-stitching dozens of tiny silk diamonds to running up an over-sized tablecloth from a bundle of vintage tea towels. I've enjoyed playing with these changes in scale and speed, and like the idea that whilst some of the projects will take many relaxing hours to stitch, others can be completed in an afternoon.

Appliqué is patchwork's sister craft, and instead of sewing the fabric together, cut-out shapes are sewn, or patched, on to a background. I've always felt like a virtuous homemaker when doing any domestic repairs, so I've even included some proper patching – a simple square on a worn-out knee. There are more involved techniques too, like the beautiful 'Hidden Circles' pattern used for the hand-appliquéd laundry bag on pages 58–61 and the intricate embroidered jigsaw of 'Crazy Patchwork' used on the cushion on pages 82–85.

I wanted to include something for everybody, so whatever your level of expertise, I hope you'll find a project that you'll enjoy making. My own first patchwork project was worked with paper templates, in English style, so maybe the Child's Pentagon Ball on pages 98–103 or the Hexagon Pincushion on pages 134–137 would make a good starting point for hand stitching. Moving on to machined patchwork, there's a range of pretty and practical bags, embellished garments and home accessories. You'll find cushions of all shapes and sizes, two full-size bedcovers, a curtain panel and a comfortable beanbag made out of plaid blankets.

The thrill of searching for vintage fabrics at boot sales and flea markets has long been one of my greatest pleasures, and I've always loved collecting textile scraps. Patchwork is the ideal way to use these: shirtings, silk scarves, dress prints, fine cotton, ticking and embroidered linen all appear alongside my own prints, and the more eclectic and unexpected the combination of fabrics, the better the result.

My intention in this book has been to broaden the boundaries of traditional patchwork and to take it back to its early roots by re-using fabric in innovative ways. Search through your ragbag for hoarded scraps, look through the following pages, and be inspired.

Cath Kidson

Patch! Basics

This introduction includes all the stitchery skills you'll need to create the projects, along with hints and tips on choosing equipment, using a sewing machine and finding fabrics, as well as some background to the various patchwork and appliqué techniques involved.

Essential Equipment

One of the best things about patchwork and appliqué is that you don't need any specialist equipment to get started. Here's a guide to the tools and equipment that you'll need to make the projects in this book – the 'sewing kit' that appears in each materials checklist.

PINNING AND STITCHING

Keep all your hand-sewing needles together in the felt pages of a needle book, where they are easily visible – they do tend to get lost in a pincushion. They come in various lengths and thicknesses, from a chunky '1' down to a delicate size '10', each intended for a particular purpose. A mixed starter pack will contain:

• long 'embroidery' or 'crewel' needles, with narrow eyes to accommodate stranded threads

• medium-length 'sharps' for general use, which have small round eyes for sewing thread

• short 'betweens' or 'quilting' needles, slender enough to slip easily through several layers of fabric. These are also good for joining English-style paper patches but may prove too small for some stitchers.

A large safety pin or bodkin is useful for threading cords through gathering channels. Smaller safety pins are good for temporarily securing layers of fabric. Fine (0.6mm) steel dressmaker's pins are suitable for cotton and other fine fabrics as they won't leave marks, but I prefer longer glass-headed pins, which show up well, especially on woollens and patterned cloth. Store them safely in a tin or pincushion, but have a small magnet to hand in case they go astray.

MEASURING AND MARKING

All stitchers need an accurate tape measure, and if you're going to make quilts or curtains, an extra long one is invaluable. Use a 15cm ruler for checking seam allowances and hems. A sharp HB pencil is all you need for transferring markings and outlines, but you may prefer a dressmaker's pen. Use tailor's chalk or a chalk pencil on textured and darker fabrics.

CUTTING OUT

Invest in the best steel-bladed scissors you can afford and they'll last you a lifetime. Dressmaking shears are useful for cutting out large items, but smaller scissors are good for patches. Keep a spare pair of household scissors for paper and don't ever use your fabric scissors for templates or they will quickly become blunt! Embroidery scissors with sharp points will snip seams and threads efficiently. Most patchworkers also have a rotary cutter, quilter's ruler and a cutting mat – you can learn more about these overleaf.

SEWING AND TACKING

Stock up with spools of white and mid-grey thread for piecing different fabrics and a couple of bright colours for tacking, so stitches are easy to spot and unpick. All-purpose sewing thread is good for hand or machine piecing. It comes in a wide range of colours – pick a slightly darker shade if you can't find an exact match for your fabric. Buy a thread plait, made from many short interwoven lengths, so that you'll always have the right colour for small sewing tasks.

ODDS AND ENDS

A thimble is essential if you're to avoid punctures when hand sewing. Silicone versions mould to your finger tip and are easier to use than traditional metal. Seam rippers are indispensible for unpicking stitches when things go wrong. A lint roller is handy for picking up threads and slivers of fabric. Finally, an old-fashioned block of beeswax for strengthening thread adds a sweet scent to your sewing kit.

Cutting Out

Whether you are preparing the panels of a cushion cover or a stack of patches ready for a quilt, accurate measurement and precise cutting are essential if your completed project is going to have a professional finish with the pieces joined correctly together.

PAPER PATTERNS

If you are making up a bag, cushion or pillowslip, you'll need rectangular panels of various sizes for the straps, gussets, lining and backings, as well as the elements needed for the patchwork or appliqué. The dimensions for each panel are given in the 'cutting out' list for the project. When two measurements are given for a rectangular piece of fabric, the width measurement is always given first, then the length. Transfer these measurements on to dressmaker's pattern paper, which is ruled with a grid of centimetre squares, then cut out along the printed lines. Pin the patterns to your fabric and cut out around the outside edge with your largest scissors. When measurements are given for individual patches, as for the curtain or washbag, draw your pattern up on 1mm grid graph paper in the same way.

If making a large backing for a finished quilt, it's easier to lay the fabric out flat and pin the quilt top to it, then cut the edge. This way you'll know they fit together exactly and there's no measuring up to do.

TEMPLATES

On the template sheets you'll find the templates required for many of the patchwork and appliqué projects, including several geometric shapes alongside the 'Dresden Plate' petals used in the bag and cushion. There is an appliqué Stanley and a couple of rabbits, plus the embroidery guide for the red work hens.

The geometric shapes are a pentagon for the child's toy ball on pages 98–103, a hexagon for the pincushion on pages 134–137 and a diamond for the Harlequin Bag on page 46–49. All of these are made using the English patchwork technique of stitching over paper templates. The best way to make the templates is to photocopy the page on to thin card, then cut out the shape. Draw round this card shape on to scrap paper. Make your own templates in other sizes by adjusting the size on your printer, using a simple drawing programme on your computer, or with a bit of geometry, a ruler and a pair of compasses.

The outline template supplied for the Bunny Sweater on pages 148–149 is intended for iron-on appliqué, so trace the reversed silhouette directly on to the paper side of the fusible bonding web. The motif for the Bunny Blanket on pages 106–107 and the Stanley appliqué for the Personalised Dog Bed on page 138–143 are stitched on to their backgrounds and are the right way round. Trace them onto kitchen paper and cut out around the pencil line to make the templates.

GO WITH THE GRAIN

Press the fabric well before cutting, to remove the creases. A light spray of starch or silicone fabric stiffener should get rid of any that are stubborn. Look hard and you'll see it's made up from two sets of interwoven threads which lie at right angles to each other. These are called the warp and weft, and the direction in which they lie is called the 'grain' of the fabric. Always position your templates so that the straight edges lie parallel with one set of threads (along the grain), or the patches will distort and pull when stitched together.

PLANNING YOUR PATCHES

If your fabric prints have an all-over, small-scale

pattern the placement of the templates isn't important, because all the patches will be more or less the same. When working with stripes and checks, however, you should plan the positioning more carefully, so that one edge of the patch is in line with the stripes or squares. You may also want the patches to be symmetrical or matching, which will require extra fabric.

Pick out individual motifs or flower sprays from other larger-scale or sprigged designs, centering them within the patch, as for the flowered silks for the Boudoir Cushion on pages 78–81 and the nursery prints on the Pentagon Ball on pages 98–103. If you make them all the same (known as 'fussy cutting') you can create some very interesting effects.

Organise your prepared patches in zip-up sandwich bags, and if you're feeling efficient, label them too.

ROTARY CUTTING

This relatively new innovation speeds the cutting out process, especially when making a large project like the Star Throw on pages 108–113 or the Curtain Panel on pages 116–121. It enables you to cut several layers of fabric at once. Three separate tools are required:

• A rotary cutter, which acts like a very sharp pastry wheel. There are several types and sizes, but all have a round, rotating blade set in a handle. A 45mm diameter is best for patchwork. Check that it can be securely retracted to prevent accidents and always handle with care.

• A quilter's ruler, made from clear perspex and etched with a grid of centimetres or inches. The largest size, used for panels and extra large patches, is 15 x 60cm. Along with a 15cm square that is marked with 45 degree angle (for triangles), this should cover most of your needs. Glue small strips of fine sand paper to the back of the ruler to stop it slipping.

• A cutting mat, with a self-healing plastic surface. If you have space, get one to cover the table top. The extra expense is worth it in the long run.

There are two ways to rotary cut and it's a good idea to practise on some spare fabric first, to get the hang of the technique. For panels and larger patches, place the fabric on the mat and line up the ruler with the printed grid. Hold the cutter so that the blade is upright and lies against the ruler, then press down firmly and glide it away from you. Do the same, matching the ruler to the correct distance, on the other three sides.

You can also use the grid marked on the ruler to measure your patches. Line one corner up with the grain of the fabric and cut along these two edges. Turn the ruler the other way round, so that the lines that indicate your required size line up with the cut edges, then slice off the fabric from these two sides.

Machine
Know-how

Only a few *Patch!* projects are stitched completely by hand. All the others involve machine sewing, but don't let this put you off if you're a novice stitcher. Nothing requires a great degree of technical knowledge and there's only one curved seam in the book... everything else consists of basic straight seams and hems and you'll learn how to do these on the following pages.

CHOOSING A MACHINE
Some patchworkers like to use antique hand-operated machines, preferring the accuracy and slow rhythmic pace produced by turning the handle. The basic straight stitch made by an old Singer is all you really need to join patches.

Modern machines, however, have a swing needle which moves from side to side to create zigzag and overlocking stitches. These are useful for neatening and strengthening raw seams and for edging appliqué patches. Any other functions are a bonus, so if you're buying your first machine don't be tempted to overspend on a digital model that links to your laptop. A solid entry-level machine (never the very cheapest, which often are not substantial enough to deal with heavier cloth) will get you started.

THE TECHNICALITIES
All machines work in the same way by linking two threads – one on each side of the fabric – to produce an interlinked stitch. The upper reel is threaded under tension along the arm and down through the needle. The lower thread is wound onto a small bobbin housed in a case that is set into the flat bed. Read through the manufacturer's manual to learn a bit more about how to use your individual machine and to get

to know some technical terms. But these are the four main parts with which you should be familiar:

• The presser foot presses down on the fabric as it passes under the needle. It's operated by a small lever that lifts it up and down. It should always be lowered before you start stitching. You will need to change the pressure when sewing thicker fabrics and the manual will tell you where to do this. Machines are supplied with several feet – you'll need just the basic one for all your seaming and the narrow zip foot when inserting a zip or sewing piping.

• The top end of the machine needle is attached to the arm and the upper thread passes through a hole in its tip. Like sewing needles, these come in different gauges and a 'universal' 70–80 should be fine when working with cotton fabrics. You'll need to adjust the needle's position when the zip foot is in place.

• The reverse stitch control is useful as it works a few stitches in the opposite direction at the beginning and end of each seam to prevent unravelling.

• The flat throat plate has a small hole through which the needle passes to pick up the lower thread. It is engraved with a series of parallel lines: you can just see these on the photograph opposite. The adjacent figures indicate the distance between the needle and the line in millimetres, in other words, the width of the seam allowance.

LOOKING AFTER YOUR MACHINE
You'll need to do routine maintenance to keep your machine running smoothly. Always store it in the carry case or dust cover and oil occasionally as directed in the manual. Clear lint and dust from the bobbin case with the tiny brush supplied. It's a good idea to change the needle frequently as it will become blunt with use and cause the stitches to become irregular.

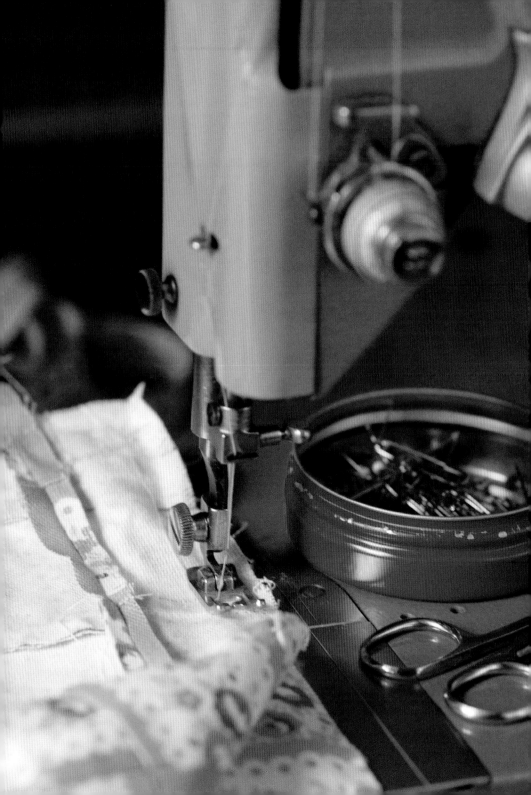

Sewing Basics

Any specialist patchwork and appliqué methods are explained in detail, with step-by-step illustrations, in the *Patch!* Projects section. Here's a quick tutorial covering the other basic sewing and finishing techniques you will need to complete the projects.

SEAMS

Whether you are joining two tiny square patches or the front and back of a pillowcase, the basic seaming method is the same. On larger panels you may be asked to neaten the edges with a zigzag or overlock stitch. Pin the two pieces with right sides facing and the raw edges and corners aligned. You can then tack larger panels if you wish, by joining with a row of long running stitches, removing the pins as you go.

STRAIGHT SEAM

Machine stitch along the specified seam allowance, using the side of the foot or the lines on the flat bed to gauge the distance between the needle and the edge. Press the seam allowance open, as shown, or press both sides to the left or right according to the instructions. This is particularly important when joining patches. Working a few stitches in the opposite direction at each end reinforces the seam.

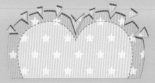

CORNER SEAM

When you come to a corner, keep the needle in the down position and lift the presser foot. Pivot the fabric and sew along the next edge. Trim the corners to within 3mm of the stitches, then turn right side out

and ease the corner into shape with a blunt pencil.

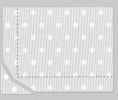

CURVED SEAM

There's only one curved seam used in all the projects, but as it's on Stanley's ear it's an important one! On an outside curve you need to reduce the amount of fabric in the allowance so that the seam will lie flat. Do this by snipping a series of evenly spaced little notches to within 2mm of the stitching, all round the curve.

CLOSING A GAP

When making a stuffed toy or the pincushion you'll need to leave a gap in a seam through which to add the filling. Press back the allowance on each side before turning through, add the filling, then pin the two edges together and slip stitch, passing the needle through the folds for a neat finish.

HEMS

A raw edge can be finished by folding it over and stitching down the turning, as around the top of the Dresden Plate Tote Bag on pages 66–69, or by covering it with a narrow length of bias binding for a more decorative look, which I did for the Circles Laundry Bag on pages 58–61.

SINGLE HEM

Neaten the edge of the fabric, if directed, then with the wrong side facing, fold the edge back to the required depth. Sometimes all you'll need to do at this stage is press it down, or you may have to machine stitch, just below the zigzag.

DOUBLE HEM

Fold and press the first turning to the given measurement, then make the second turning which may be the same or slightly deeper. Pin and tack, then machine stitch close to the inner fold or slip stitch by hand.

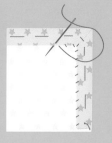

BOUND HEM

I bound the top edge of the Circles Laundry Bag on pages 58–61 by hand. Press the binding in half and slot it over the edge, tacking it down as you go. At the corners, mitre the surplus. Sew down with small stitches, catching down both folded edges at the same time.

HANDLES

This method for making fabric handles could be used instead of webbing for the Tweed Messenger Bag on pages 38–41 and the Sugarbag Doorstop on pages 124–127. Cut a strip twice the finished width, plus 2cm. Press under a 1cm turning along each long edge, then press in half. Tack edges together and machine stitch 3mm from the edge. Remove the tacking.

MITRED CORNER

To mitre the corner of a single hem, press both hems and unfold. Turn in the corner at 45 degrees and press. Trim off the corner to within 5mm of the diagonal crease, refold and stitch down.

REINFORCING STITCHING

When a handle is sewn to a bag the join has to be reinforced, so that it can bear weight. Tack one end of the handle (slightly more than its width), behind the bag. Starting at the top right corner, sew a square or rectangle of machine stitches over the top. Now sew diagonally across to bottom left, back along the bottom edge and up to the top left corner.

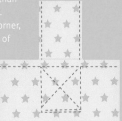

Traditional Techniques

English Patchwork was the first sewing technique that I learnt, and I will always remember the process of joining scraps of fabrics to make something new. There are four other classic hand techniques which have been adapted for this book.

ENGLISH PATCHWORK

Also known as Paper or Mosaic Patchwork, this centuries-old method is used primarily to piece accurate geometric shapes. Each patch is tacked over a paper template and the folded edges then sewn together. The aim at one time was to work 8 or 9 stitches per centimetre but we are all a little more forgiving today! A traditional way of preventing the thread from fraying as it passes repeatedly through the fabric is to draw it over a block of pure beeswax.

CRAZY PATCHWORK

The Victorians invented this extravagant patchwork style, indulging their love of ornament and decoration. They made fantastic confections of brocade, velvet and satin in deep colours and with rich textures, then encrusted them with intricate embroidery stitches. It's a combination of appliqué and patchwork, in which fragments of cloth are laid out on a plain background and are fitted together like a jigsaw to create a fragmented, crazed surface. The fabric is then stitched down and the seams embellished. I've reinterpreted this technique in a fresher, lighter way with my Crazy Patchwork Cushion on pages 82–85.

CATHEDRAL WINDOW

A relatively recent development, dating from the 1920s, the 'windows' are usually worked with a frame of white cotton and patterned diamond-shaped 'panes'. For the Boudoir Cushion on pages 78–81 I chose a vintage cream sateen as the background for a collection of pastel lingerie silk. Like the Suffolk Puff, this is a technique that's always explored further by innovative stitchers, and it works well with a darker background. There is a variation called Secret Garden, where an extra layer of fabric is placed within the folded square, just before the points are stitched down. This is revealed when the edges are turned back and adds extra colour to the inside of the petals.

SUFFOLK PUFFS

You won't fail to notice that this is my favourite technique at the moment and, as you'll see, I've actually managed to incorporate puffs into five of the projects. In the following pages they are used to make a cushion cover, to embellish a cardigan and to create a necklace... see if you can spot the other two. Sometimes called yo-yos or pom-poms, they are undergoing something of a revival at the moment. They are very versatile and quick to make. All you have to do is cut out a circle of fabric, sew down a turning all around the edge and draw up your thread to gather up the fabric. To speed up this process you can even buy clever little gadgets that help you create puffs in a range of different sizes.

HAND APPLIQUÉ

Folded edge appliqué is another technique with a long history. It involves cutting out fabric shapes, tacking a narrow hem around the edge, then sewing the patch to a background. In mid-nineteenth-century America it was used to create wonderfully colourful and ornate quilts, especially around the seaport of Baltimore. Folding narrow hems can prove fiddly, so for the Circles Laundry Bag pictured opposite and the Dresden Plate Tote Bag and Cushion on pages 66–73, you will learn how to tack the fabric over a template first to create perfect curves.

Hand Appliqué

This term derives from the French verb 'appliquer' which translates as 'to put on', consequently the technique involves cutting out small pieces of fabric and literally putting them on to a background. The traditional way of doing this by hand is explained on the previous page, but you can also attach the shapes with iron-on fusible bonding web – a much quicker method.

BONDING WEB

Fusible bonding web is a sheet of translucent paper with a backing of heat-activated adhesive. There are several types and weights sold under different trade names, but they all do the same thing. Ensure you buy the correct one for your fabric: if you use heavyweight web on silk or lawn the adhesive will show through the fine weave.

All you have to do is trace the reversed outline of the motif directly on to the paper side of the web. Cut it out roughly and with the adhesive side downwards, iron the paper to the wrong side of the appliqué fabric (following the manufacturer's guidelines). Trim precisely around the pencil line. Peel away the paper, place the motif on the background in its final position, and press with a hot iron to fuse the adhesive. Broderie Perse shapes (see below) can also be fixed with bonding web. Cut a piece that is slightly larger than your chosen part of the fabric, iron it to the wrong side, then cut around the printed outline.

EDGING YOUR MOTIFS

Your motifs are now in place but the edges are still raw, so you'll need to neaten them to stop them fraying. The functional way to do this is by machine, with a narrow, closely-spaced zigzag or with one of the more decorative stitches. Use a matching thread if you want an invisible border (like that on the Hounds Bag on pages 54–57). A hand-embroidered finish would always be my first choice however, and on pages 28–29 you'll find instructions for some of my favourite stitches.

BRODERIE PERSE

If you've ever cut out images and glued them into a scrapbook (a rainy-day pastime for most kids at some stage), you'll be familiar with the idea behind Broderie Perse. This is another French term, meaning Persian Embroidery, although it's not from Persia and it isn't really embroidery! The earliest surviving examples date from the 1600s when exotic floral chintz was first imported into England by the East India Company. Individual flowers, leaves, birds and butterflies were cut from this highly-prized fabric and then sewn on to a plain background to form new pictorial designs.

Any printed fabric can be used for Broderie Perse and you can really let your imagination run riot when it comes to collaging the motifs. I found some fabulous full-blown roses on a furnishing remnant to fill the vase in the Flower Picture, shown at almost full-size on pages 144–147. This project also incorporates vintage buttons and some hand embroidery to draw in the stems and embellish the flowers. A more random interpretation can be found on the linen Appliqué Tea Towel in the country kitchen on pages 132–133. These nostalgic designs came from a length of homemaker-style barkcloth curtaining and are edged with an unobtrusive buttonhole stitch, worked in thread to match the fabric background. The third Broderie Perse project is the Hounds Bag on pages 54–57, which recycles motifs from a much more delicate fabric – a twill silk headscarf.

Embroidery & Embellishments

Both patchwork and appliqué are so decorative in themselves that they scarcely need any more surface decoration, but sometimes an extra detail can provide the finishing touch that makes a piece really stand out. Embellishment can be understated – a line of simple stitches around a tweed patch for example – or an integral part of the overall design, like the feather stitch around the patches on the Crazy Patch Cushion.

BUTTONS

Buttons of all shapes and sizes can be used for practical purposes – fastening a pillowcase or securing a bag handle – or as pure ornament. I picked out a varied selection from my tin of vintage buttons to add highlights of colour and texture to the Flower Picture on pages 144–147. Keep an eye out for old cloth laundry buttons and those made from early plastics, wood or pressed glass. Mother-of-pearl buttons have a neutral, natural finish that goes well with any fabric and you can add extra colour by sewing them on with bright embroidery thread.

However carefully you stitch, there may be times when your seams don't line up perfectly at the corners. Joins that are not quite precise can be concealed with the careful placing of a few buttons... this secret cheat worked especially well on the Boudoir Cushion and it's also good for misaligned square patches.

LACE, RIBBON AND CORD

I'm not usually keen on a lot of frilly lace, but used with discretion it can be very effective. The centre panel of the Rose Knitting Bag on pages 50–53 is framed with a simple triangular edging, which proved the perfect counterpoint to the white rose and daisy print. In the same way the fine pink piping around the Crazy Patch Cushion on pages 82–85 picks up the colour of the embroidery thread and outlines the patchwork square.

If you don't fancy making your own piping and setting it into the seam you can simply sew a length cord or other trimming around the edge of the finished cushion. Shiny or cotton cord also makes an attractive drawstring for large and small bags, and you can finish off the ends with a few beads or a fabric tab. Ricrac is a good alternative to lace, and can be used as a border or inserted in seams to give a discreet scalloped finish. Children's garments are an exception to minimalism and a ribbon bow gives character to the Bunny Sweater on pages 148–149.

STITCHERY

You can create some interesting embellishments with just a few hand embroidery stitches, all of which are shown on the next two pages. Edge appliqué patches with blanket or coral stitch and cover plain seams with feather and fly stitches. Personalise your projects with a monogram worked in back stitch or chain stitch. I have just discovered figural red work embroidery which I chose for the embroidered Red Hens Bag on pages 42–45.

There are several ways to transfer the hen or any other photocopied outline on to fabric. The simplest is to use dressmaker's carbon paper. Sandwich together the fabric, the face-down carbon, then the photocopy, taping down each layer so they don't shift. Draw firmly over the outline with a ballpoint pen. Alternatively you can improvise a light box. Masking tape the outline to a bright window, tape the fabric to the paper and trace the outline with a sharp pencil.

Embroidery Stitches

All the embroidery in this book is worked with a long-eyed needle and stranded embroidery cotton or tapestry yarn. Both threads come in a skein that is held together with one wide and one narrow paper band. Hold on to the narrow band and pull the loose end of the thread gently to withdraw it, then cut off a 45cm length. Stranded embroidery cotton is made up of six loosely twisted threads, which can easily be separated. Six strands gives bold stitches, three a medium line, whilst two create a much finer effect. The project steps will always tell you how many to use.

RUNNING STITCH

This basic stitch is used in English patchwork for tacking fabric to templates and on a smaller scale, for quilting. The stitches should all be the same length, as should the spaces between them.

BACK STITCH

Bring the needle up one stitch length from the beginning of the line, then take it back to the start point. Come up again one stitch length ahead of this first stitch and continue, keeping the stitches regular.

STRAIGHT STITCH

Tiny upright or angled straight stitches can be used to anchor appliqué patches or to add small details. Simply come up at A and down again at B to make a short straight line.

SATIN STITCH

So called because of its smooth, shiny finish, this consists of a series of straight stitches worked alongside each other in the same direction, from A to B. Vary the lengths to fill the shape being worked.

BLANKET STITCH

This classic edging stitch is used to neaten the edge of the motifs. Come up at A, then take the needle up to B, through the fabric and out directly below at C. Finally loop the thread under the needle and pull it through. Repeat this sequence to the end.

TAILOR'S BUTTONHOLE STITCH

A reinforced version of blanket stitch. Starting at A, take the needle down at B, in front of the thread and bring the point through at C. Loop the thread from left to right and pull through, lifting the needle so that the thread forms a small knot at the edge of the motif.

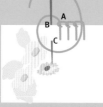

CHAIN STITCH

Use this for flexible wide outlines and for monograms or other lettering. Bring the needle out at A, then reinsert it in the same place. Bring the point out at B and loop the thread from left to right under the needle. Hold the loop down and pull the needle through gently to draw up the thread. Finish with a straight stitch over the last loop.

LAZY DAISY STITCH

Single chain stitches make good petals but I worked a few long thin ones to make the tuft at the top of the Blanket Bunny's carrot! Work as for chain stitch, anchoring each loop with a short straight stitch.

SINGLE FEATHER STITCH

This is a variation on blanket stitch and is used to edge circular patches. Come up at A and insert the needle at B. Bring the point out at C, below B and in line with A. Loop the thread under the needle and pull through.

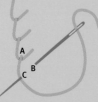

FEATHER STITCH

This pretty stitch is used to embroider the Crazy Patch Cushion on pages 82–85. Keep all the stitches the same length and at the same angle on either side for a neat appearance. Come up at A and take it down at B forming a loose stitch. Bring the point out at C, over the thread and pull through. Work the next angled stitch from D to E over the looped thread. Repeat these two stitches to the end.

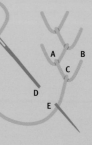

FLY STITCH

This is another good stitch to work over seams. Come up at A and take the needle back down at B, then back up at an angle, at C. Pull through over the thread and go down again, directly below at D. Repeat this stitch to form a continuous row.

Choosing Fabrics

When it comes to selecting fabrics for patchwork and appliqué, you'll find the choice is limitless! Specialist quilt shops and department stores are piled high with rolls of new cloth and are a good source of remnants and fat quarters (the quilter's term for a 55 x 50cm rectangle). Also, search charity shops, flea markets and even the back of your own wardrobe for old fabrics to recycle in true patchwork tradition. For the items in this book I've used everything from silk scarves and tablecloths to hand-woven tweed and antique curtain material. The following guidelines will help you pick the right fabric for your projects.

VINTAGE TEXTILES
Almost any vintage fabric can be used, as long as it is in good condition. Check carefully for stains, rust-marks or signs of wear and cut away these areas. Hold the fabric up to the light to check where the threads have worn thin. Even if it appears to be in good condition, launder first – the fabric often needs freshening and if it can stand up to a gentle machine wash, it will be strong enough to sew.

COTTON AND LINEN
There is a wealth of wonderful domestic linen out there that's just waiting for you to come along: look out for hand-embroidered napkins, runners, pillowcases and dressing table mats. Fine quality sheets make good backings for projects and even humble stripey tea towels come into their own when patched together to make a tablecloth. Printed versions are a good alternative to buying wider and more expensive fabrics.

SILKS AND WOOLLENS
The rich textures of velvet, satin and silk add another dimension to patchwork, but these fabrics aren't always easy to work with. Delicate silk patches need to be backed with interfacing to hold their shape or combined with firmer fabrics. The 'Cathedral Window' technique used for the Boudoir Cushion on pages 78–81 is a good example of how to do this. Projects like floor cushions, that will get a lot of hard use, need to be made from larger patches of thicker materials, so old blankets are ideal for these (especially if you've had moths in the house).

PRINTS AND PATTERNS
Small-scale floral dress fabrics are the classic choice for patchwork, and work best when a few plain colours are thrown into the blend. You can mix large and small prints with checks and ginghams, but try to keep within a limited colour palette as I did for the Child's Cushion on pages 94–97, or the overall effect can be a bit overwhelming. I particularly like working with printed or woven stripes, cutting them into square or rectangular patches, then reassembling them to make new geometric patterns.

'Fussy cut' patches of patterned fabrics, like those I made for the Hexagon Pincushion on pages 134–137, create rhythmic repeating designs or you can select interesting individual motifs for appliqué patches – I couldn't resist the nostalgic racing cars used on the Patched Dungarees on pages 150–151. For the framed Flower Picture on pages 144–147 I cut out a series of large rose motifs from glazed chintz and stitched them to a length of plain damask – an old technique called Broderie Perse first used when new fabrics were scarce and costly.

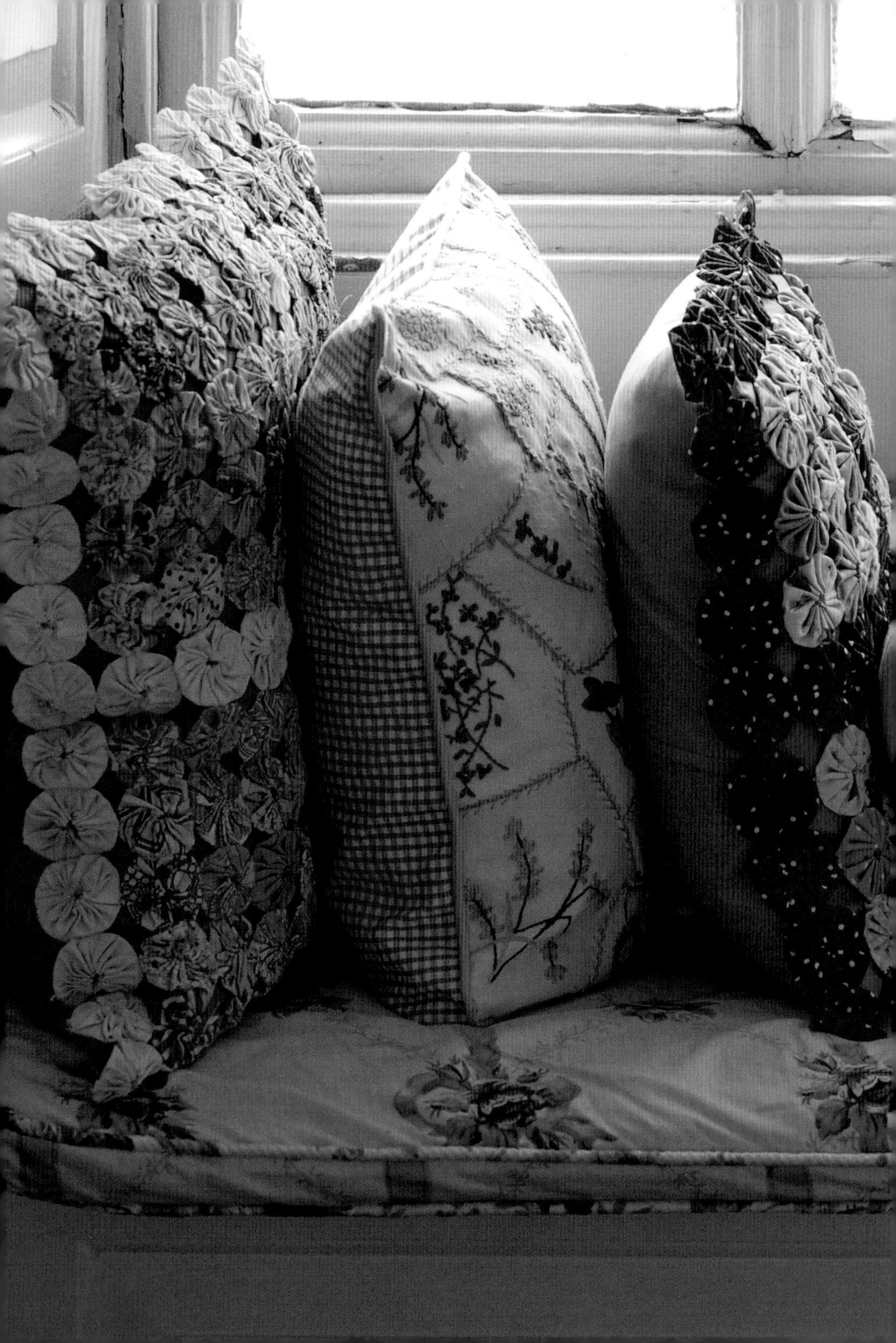

Patch! Projects

Designing the projects for this book, selecting the perfect fabrics and deciding exactly which techniques to use, was a hugely enjoyable task. Whether you're a needlework novice or an experienced stitcher, I hope you'll enjoy them as much as I have done.

Floral & Spot
Tote Bag

MATERIALS

• 140 x 70cm spot print fabric • 140 x 40cm floral print fabric • stranded embroidery thread in red • matching sewing thread • sewing machine • sewing kit

CUTTING

from spot print fabric • seventeen 12cm squares • two 52 x 32cm lining panels • one 42 x 12cm lining base
from floral print fabric • seventeen 12cm squares • one 22 x 12cm pocket • two 60 x 8cm handle strips

Here's a relaxed and roomy bag. It's made from one of my favourite fabric combinations – spots and flowers – and I love the contrast between bold dots and delicate briar roses.

The seam allowance throughout is 1cm.

1 Lay 30 squares in a chequered pattern, in three rows of 10. Right sides facing, sew in vertical rows of three, see page 20.

2 For each row with a spot square at the top and bottom, press the seams upwards and for each with a floral square at the top and bottom, press downwards.

3 Join the rows to make a rectangle. Right sides facing, match the long seam edges. Insert a pin at each seam line and at the top and bottom corners, then machine stitch.

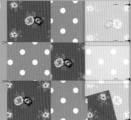

4 Press all the vertical seams open. Seam and press the two side edges to make a cylinder of patchwork. Now press.

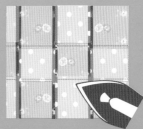

5 Sew the remaining four squares together to make the base, alternating the spot and floral prints. Press the seams open.

6 With right sides facing inwards, pin one long edge of the bag base to four squares along the bottom edge of the main bag, matching the open seams. Pin the other long edge to the opposite side of the bag, leaving the short edges open. Make a 5mm snip into the bottom of each corner seam to open out. Machine stitch the two seams, starting and finishing each line of stitching 1cm from the short edge and working a few backwards stitches to strengthen.

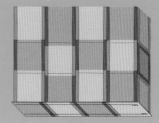

top tip I'LL LET YOU INTO A SECRET... THIS BAG IS ACTUALLY MADE FROM FOUR COTTON TEA TOWELS, ALWAYS A GREAT SOURCE OF NEW FABRIC IN SMALLER QUANTITIES!

Floral & Spot
Tote Bag

7 Pin the short edges of the base to the bag and machine stitch. Work two more rounds of stitching over to reinforce the seam.

8 Using a thick crewel needle and 3 strands of red embroidery thread, work a line of running stitch, 5mm in from each side seam.

9 Neaten the top edge of the pocket with a double hem. Press under a 1cm turning along the other three sides. Pin the pocket to one lining panel, 6cm down from the top edge and 11cm in from the left side edge. Machine in place, working extra stitches at the beginning and end of the seam.

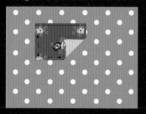

10 Right sides facing, join the lining to make a cylinder. Press the seams open, then a 15mm turning around the top edge. Make a 6mm snip into the seam allowance at each

corner. Right sides facing, pin the base, lining up opposite corners to the two seams. Double stitch into place.

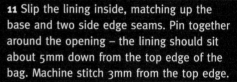

11 Slip the lining inside, matching up the base and two side edge seams. Pin together around the opening – the lining should sit about 5mm down from the top edge of the bag. Machine stitch 3mm from the top edge.

12 Press each handle strip in half widthways and unfold. Press a 1cm turning each of the four edges, then re-press the centre crease. Machine stitch 3mm from each long edge. Tack the ends of the handles to the sides of the bag so that they lie 5cm down from the top edge and overlap the side patchwork seams. Sew down with rectangles of reinforcing stitch (see page 21).

top tip LINES OF TOP STITCHING ALONG EACH SIDE SEAM DEFINE THE SHAPE OF THE BAG. TO MAKE THEM STAND OUT, MATCH THE COLOUR OF THE THREAD TO THE FABRIC: I CHOSE A WARM RED THAT HIGHLIGHTS THE ROSE DETAIL.

Tweed
Messenger Bag

MATERIALS

• eighteen 14cm squares tweed fabric • tapestry yarn in shades to match • large crewel needle • 72 x 38cm cotton fabric for lining • 125cm of 5cm-wide webbing for bag handle • matching sewing thread • quilter's ruler • chalk pencil • sewing machine • sewing kit

There's plenty of space in this over-shoulder messenger bag for all your daily essentials. It's quick to make from simple squares of tweed. Each patch is outlined with a round of running stitches worked in tapestry yarn and the one in the centre is monogrammed.

1 Using a quilter's ruler and chalk pencil, mark a guide on each tweed square, 2cm in from the edge. Thread the crewel needle with tapestry yarn to match each colour in turn, and sew a line of small running stitches around every chalk outline.

2 Arrange the first nine squares in three horizontal rows of three, moving them about until you have a balanced arrangement of colour and pattern.

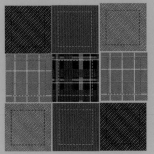

3 Draw your initials on the centre square using the chalk pencil. Embroider over the lines with small back stitches (see page 20).

4 Join the squares in horizontal rows, starting at the bottom left corner. Pin the right edge of the first square to the left edge of the second square and machine stitch with a 12mm seam allowance. Repeat with the third square. Press the two seams towards the left.

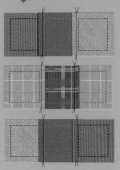

5 Join the three centre squares and press the seams to the right, then sew the top three squares together and press the seam towards the left.

top tip   I MADE MY BAG WITH A PATCHWORK PANEL AT BOTH FRONT AND BACK, BUT YOU COULD USE A SINGLE LARGE SQUARE OF TWEED TO MAKE A PLAIN REVERSE SIDE. A SMALL MONOGRAM IN THE CORNER WOULD PROVIDE EXTRA VISUAL INTEREST.

Tweed Messenger Bag

6 With right sides facing, pin the bottom edge of the top row to the top edge of the centre row so that the seams match up. Insert a pin at both points where the seams meet and at each corner. Machine stitch leaving a 12mm allowance. Add the bottom row in the same way and press all the horizontal seams upwards.

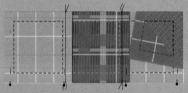

7 Sew the nine remaining squares together in the same way to make the back of the bag. Press the horizontal seams upwards. Pin the side and bottom edges of the front and back together with right sides facing, once again matching the corners and seams.

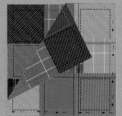

8 Machine stitch 12mm from the edge, then stitch over the line once again to reinforce. Clip a small triangle from each bottom corner so that they will lie flat (see page 21). Turn the bag right side out, ease out the corners and press lightly.

9 Neaten the top edge by turning back and tacking down a 12mm turning. You will need to open out the seams as you go, so that the opening doesn't become too lumpy.

10 Pin the handle ends to the inside top corners of the bag, overlapping by 5cm. The seams should lie halfway across the webbing. Tack and machine stitch a rectangle of reinforcing stitches (see page 21).

11 Fold the lining in half, right sides facing. Pin and machine stitch the two sides with a 1cm seam, then press a 3cm turning around the opening. Slip into the bag. Pin the folded edge 5mm below the top of the bag, then slip stitch it in place.

top tip IF YOU CAN'T FIND THE PERFECT EDGING, DON'T FORGET THAT YOU CAN ALWAYS CUSTOMISE. THIS FURNISHING FRINGE COMPLEMENTED THE CUSHIONS PERFECTLY, BUT IT WAS A BIT TOO LONG... SO I SIMPLY TRIMMED IT DOWN WITH MY SHARPEST SCISSORS!

Red Hens
Bag

MATERIALS

• 1m x 80cm red cotton fabric • 80 x 15cm white linen fabric • 1m x 50cm striped cotton fabric • 2m of 2.5cm-wide white bias binding • off-white and red stranded cotton embroidery thread • four 2.5cm buttons • matching sewing thread • sewing machine • sewing kit

CUTTING OUT

from red cotton fabric • two 10 x 41cm side gussets • one 10 x 38cm bottom gusset • one 38 x 41cm back panel • two 8 x 70cm straps • two 8 x 15cm tabs

from striped fabric • two 38 x 41cm side panels • two 10 x 41cm side gussets • one 10 x 38cm bottom gusset

Redwork embroidery – outline drawings stitched on to a plain white background – was hugely popular at the turn of the nineteenth century. Over a hundred years on, it's undergoing a revival. The embroideries have long been combined with crimson cloth to make striking, graphic patchwork.

The seam allowance throughout is 1cm.

1 Using the template, trace two left-facing and two right-facing hens within their boxes on to the white fabric (see page 26). Leave at least 6cm between each image. Stitch the outlines in small back stitches, using three strands of thread, and embroider the frames in feather stitch (see pages 30 and 31).

2 Trace the rectangle five times on to the red fabric and feather stitch in off-white around each outline, using three strands of thread.

3 Trim each completed patch down to 14cm wide by 15cm tall, making sure that there is an equal margin around the feather stitching.

4 Arrange the patches in three rows of three, alternating red and white, and with all the chickens facing as shown. With right sides facing, pin the side edges of the first two patches in the top row together and machine stitch.

5 Add the third patch to the other side of the chicken, then join the other two rows. Press all the seams towards the red patches.

6 Pin the bottom edge of the top row and the top edge of the centre row together, with right sides facing, so that the seam allowances all butt up against each other. Insert the pins along the seam lines and at both corners. Machine stitch. Repeat with the bottom row. Press the seams open.

7 Right sides facing, pin the short ends of the side gussets to the bottom making a long strip. Machine stitch, starting and finishing 1cm from the end of each seam line.

top tip FOR A FIXED, RATHER THAN AN ADJUSTABLE, HANDLE MAKE THE STRAP 10CM LONGER AND SEW THE ENDS TO THE SIDE GUSSETS OF THE BAG. YOU COULD ALWAYS ADD THE BUTTONS AS A DECORATIVE FEATURE.

Red Hens Bag

8 Right sides together, pin one long edge of the completed gusset strip to the side and bottom edges of the back panel. Open out the unstitched ends so that it fits neatly around the bottom corners. Tack in place then machine stitch, working an extra row at each corner to reinforce. Repeat with the front panel. Turn the bag right side out and press the seams lightly. Press under a 1cm turning around the opening.

9 Make up the striped lining the same way as the bag, but don't turn it through. Press back a 1.5cm turning around the top edge.

10 Trim one end of each of the four strap and tab pieces into a shallow curve. Press under a 1cm turning around each piece. Press the bias binding in half widthways.

11 Tack the binding to the wrong side of the long and curved edges of one strap and one tab so 5mm overlaps to the right side. Tack the second strap and tab in place so the binding is sandwiched between them and machine stitch 3mm from the edge. Make two buttonholes, by hand or machine, 5cm and 10cm from the end of the strap. They should lie parallel to the long edges.

12 Pin and tack the strap to the left side gusset, so that 3cm lies inside the main bag. Attach the tab to the right side in the same way, then slip in the lining. Match the seams and pin together so that the top edge of the lining lies 5mm below the opening. Hand stitch the two together, making sure that the needle goes through the turned back hem around the main bag only, and the stitches don't show on the right side. Work extra stitches along the base of the strap and tab, or sew a rectangle of machine reinforcing stitches (see page 21) at the top of each side gusset.

13 Finish off by sewing two of the buttons to the tab 5cm apart, and the other pair to the side gusset, also 5cm apart.

---

top tip ADAPT THIS IDEA TO MAKE AN AUTOGRAPH BAG AS AN END-OF-TERM SOUVENIR: GET YOUR BEST FRIENDS TO SIGN FEATHER-STITCH TRIMMED PATCHES AND BACK STITCH OVER THEIR WRITING.

Harlequin Bag

MATERIALS

• remnants of velvet and silk fabrics in a range of colours • lightweight iron-on interfacing • 1.5m of 5mm cord
• 65 x 25cm toning velvet fabric • 13cm circle of medium-weight card • matching sewing thread • glue stick
• sewing machine • scrap paper

CUTTING OUT

from toning velvet fabric • two 15cm circles for bag base and lining base • 43 x 23cm rectangle for lining

I made this diamond drawstring bag from a collection of antique silk and velvet scraps. It is perfect for your treasured possessions.

1 Following the manufacturer's instructions, strengthen silk fabrics by fusing lightweight iron-on interfacing to the wrong side.

2 You need 139 diamonds, 135 for the bag and 4 for the tabs. Cut 139 backing papers using the template and tack a fabric patch over each, allowing a 6mm seam and mitring the corners neatly (see page 23).

3 Sew the patches together in fifteen diagonal rows of nine diamonds.

4 Join the rows to make a long rectangle.

5 Right sides facing, sew the two short edges of the rectangle together to make into a cylinder.

6 Press lightly from the wrong side, then unpick all the tacking papers. Fold back and tack down the top halves of the diamonds at the top and bottom to give a straight edge around each opening.

7 Divide the bottom edge into four equal sections by inserting four pins into the fold, with three and a three-quarter patches between them. This will help you gather the edge evenly when you sew on the base.

8 Draw two lines across the cardboard circle, dividing it into quarter sections. Sew a line of long running stitches 5mm from the edge of one velvet circle. Coat the back of the card lightly with a glue stick and place it centrally on the wrong side of the velvet. Gather up the thread so that the edge covers the card and fasten off securely. Insert four pins into the card, one at the end of each line.

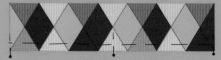

top tip YOU CAN JOIN THE DIAMONDS RANDOMLY, OR LAY THEM ALL OUT FIRST, IN FIFTEEN DIAGONAL ROWS OF NINE AND
SHUFFLE THEM AROUND TO CREATE A MORE BALANCED ARRANGEMENT.

Harlequin Bag

9 Sew a line of running stitch 5mm from the bottom edge and draw up until the opening is 1cm smaller in diameter than the velvet base. Centrally pin the base to the gathered opening – this can be awkward, so you need to 'stab' the pins through the edge of the velvet and the patchwork. Slip stitch the base to the bag with matching thread.

10 Right sides facing, pin the two short edges of the velvet rectangle together and join with a 1cm seam. Press back a 1cm turning around the top edge. Pin eight pins around the bottom edge at equal intervals.

11 Fold the remaining velvet circle in half, then quarters and position a pin at each fold. Now add another pin between each pair, to divide the circumference in eight equal sections. Right sides facing, tack the base to the bag, matching the pins. Machine stitch 1cm from the edge and trim the seam allowance back to 6mm.

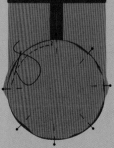

12 Sit the lining inside the bag and line up and pin the top edges together exactly. Join together by hand, with a round of slip stitch.

13 To make the drawstring channel, machine two parallel rounds of straight stitch around the opening, 2.5 and 5cm down from the top edge. Unpick one of the diagonal lines of hand stitching between these two rows and secure the other ends of the seams with a few extra stitches. Make the other opening directly opposite, in the same way.

14 Cut the cord in half and secure one end to an elastic threader or safety pin. Feed it through one opening, all the way around the channel, then out of the opening. Thread the remaining half through the other opening.

15 Tie both cords together in an overhand knot, about 10cm from the ends. Trim to 6cm. Fold one of the last diamonds in half lengthways and hold it over one cord so that the raw end is completely enclosed. Slip stitch the edges together, stab stitching through the cord. Unpick the tacking. Do the same on the other three ends.

top tip CHECK ANTIQUE FABRICS FOR ANY DAMAGED AREAS THAT MIGHT NOT BE STRONG ENOUGH FOR RE-USE. IF YOU HOLD THEM UP TO THE LIGHT YOU CAN EASILY DETECT ANY WORN PATCHES.

Rose
Knitting Bag

MATERIALS

• 70 x 25cm red floral print fabric • 120 x 50cm green spot print fabric • 1m narrow lace • pair of bag handles
• matching sewing thread • pencil and ruler • sewing machine

CUTTING OUT

from red floral print fabric • one 27 x 17cm centre flower panel • ten 7cm squares
from green spot print fabric • fourteen 7cm squares • three 37 x 27cm main panels (one for the outer bag,
two for the lining) • two 7 x 85cm side gussets (one for the outer bag, one for the lining) • four 5 x 8cm
handle loops

Vintage furnishing fabrics, like the classic rose curtain I found for this cheerful knitting bag, are ideal for patchwork projects. The triangular lace trimming frames the centre panel perfectly, echoing the shape and colour of the petals.

The seam allowance throughout is 1cm.

1 Start by joining the squares. Right sides facing, sew four spot and three floral patches together for the top and bottom strips, alternating the fabrics. Sew two floral patches to one spot square for each edge strip. Press all the seam allowances towards the floral squares.

2 Using a sharp pencil and a ruler, draw a diagonal line across the wrong side of the remaining four spot squares. Pin one to each corner of the flower panel with the line running from edge to edge. Machine stitch

along the lines, then trim the surplus fabric leaving a 1cm allowance on each seam. Press the seams towards the centre flower panel.

3 Right sides facing, pin and stitch the two three-patch edge strips to the side edges of the centre flower panel. Press the seams towards the centre. Pin on the top and bottom patchwork strips, matching the seams and corners. Machine stitch, then press the seams inwards.

4 Draw a diagonal line across each bottom corner square and cut across these marks. Pin the finished patchwork panel to one of the green spot main panels and snip a triangle from each bottom corner so that the two are the same size. Do the same with the other two main panels. Mark the 1cm seam allowance along the side and bottom edges of all four main panels.

top tip   IF YOU ARE USING A PIECE OF OLD FABRIC, HOLD IT UP TO THE LIGHT TO CHECK FOR SMALL HOLES OR ANY PARTS THAT HAVE WORN TOO THIN FOR USE. MARK THESE WITH STICKY LABELS AND CUT YOUR PATCHES FROM THE SOUND AREAS.

Rose Knitting Bag

5 Right sides facing, pin a side gusset strip to the side of the patchwork main panel. Machine stitch along the line, as far as the corner. Sew reverse stitches to secure. Snip the thread and remove the fabric from the machine. Make an 8mm cut into the seam allowance of the side, in line with the end.

6 Swivel the gusset round so the edge lies along the diagonal corner and pin the two layers together. Machine stitch along the line, just as far as the next angle. Snip the allowance again, then sew the bottom edge and the second corner in the same way. Trim the end of the gusset in line with the top edge.

7 Sew a green panel to the other edge of the side gusset to complete the outer bag. Turn right side out, ease out the corners and press the seams lightly. Press under and tack down a 1cm turning around the opening.

8 Press under a 1cm turning on each edge of the handle loops. Thread through the holes in the handles. Line up the bottom edges.

9 Position a handle so that it lies centrally along the bag front panel. Pin, then tack the bottom edges of the handle loops to the wrong side of the opening, so that 2cm projects above the top edge. Tack the other handle to the back panel in the corresponding position.

10 Using the remaining two green spot main panels and side gusset, make up the lining and press the opening as for the main bag, but don't turn it through. Slip the lining into the bag. Match up the side seams and the top edges precisely. Tack the two together and machine stitch around the top edge, 3mm from the opening.

11 Slip stitch the lace around the edge of the centre flower panel. Neaten the end by trimming it to 6mm, folding it back and stitching down.

top tip I REALLY LIKED THESE TRANSPARENT BAG HANDLES, WHICH ARE UNDERSTATED AND DON'T DOMINATE THE PRETTY PRINTS. INSTEAD OF INTRODUCING ANOTHER COLOUR, NATURAL BAMBOO WOULD MAKE A GOOD ALTERNATIVE IF YOU CAN'T FIND ANYTHING SIMILAR.

MATERIALS

• 70 x 90cm striped canvas fabric • 75 x 50cm floral print fabric for lining • old silk scarf or printed fabric
• fusible bonding web • matching sewing thread • sewing machine • sewing kit

CUTTING OUT

from striped fabric (the stripes should run vertically on each piece) • one 35 x 90cm rectangle for main bag
• two 10 x 42cm side gussets • two 8 x 60cm straps
from floral print lining fabric • two 35 x 47cm rectangles

Appliqué patches can be made from all kinds of unexpected fabrics, and I'm always on the look out for illustrative one-off prints. These four perky hounds started out on a vintage silk headscarf. Fine fabric needs reinforcement if it is to withstand everyday wear and tear, so a fusible bonding web was used to fix them on to canvas, and the raw edges were reinforced with machine stitch.

1 Decide which motifs you wish to use and plan their positions on the bag. Cut them out roughly and iron the fusible web onto the wrong side, following the manufacturer's instructions. Cut around the outlines and peel off the backing papers.

2 Fold the bag in half widthways and insert a pin at each side edge to mark the centre.

3 Fold up the top 41cm – this will be the front of the bag. Arrange the motifs as you wish, remembering to leave at least 5cm at the top edge, then iron them in place. Work a round of 3mm wide machine blanket or zigzag stitches around the edge of each shape in matching thread.

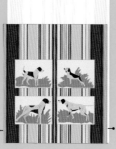

4 Mark the centre bottom edge of the two side gussets with pins. With right sides facing, place one gusset across the bag, matching the pin to the centre point of the bag.

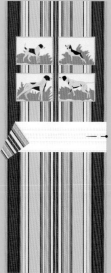

5 Make two 8mm snips into the seam allowance of the bag, 1cm in from each side edge of the gusset, so that it will fold around the corners. Pin the side edges of the bag to the sides of the gusset.

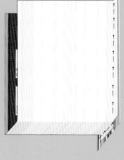

top tip — YOU WILL NEED TO ALLOW MORE FABRIC TO MAKE A SYMMETRICALLY STRIPED BAG AND TO MATCH THE SIDE GUSSETS
AND STRAPS. THIS EXTRA AMOUNT WILL DEPEND ON THE WIDTH OF THE REPEAT.

55

Hounds Bag

6 Machine stitch the bag to the gusset with a 1cm seam. Work three short diagonal lines of stitching across the corners to reinforce them, then trim the seam allowance at the corner back to 4mm (see page 20). Join the other gusset in the same way.

7 Press the seams open. Press back a 2cm turning around the opening. Turn right side out and ease the corners into right angles.

8 Pin the two lining pieces together with right sides facing and machine stitch around the side and bottom edges leaving a 1cm seam allowance. Press the seams open.

9 Now make a t-junction seam at each bottom corner to give depth to the lining. Fold it so that one side seam lies along the bottom seam. Draw an 8cm line across the corner, then machine stitch along this line. Trim the seam back to 4mm. Do the same at the other corner, then press back a 3.5mm turning around the top edge.

10 Slip the lining inside the bag, matching up the side seams. Pin the two together so that the lining lies 3mm below the top edge of the bag. Machine stitch 5mm from the top edge.

11 To make up the straps, press under a 1cm turning along each short, then each long edge of the two strips. Press them in half with wrong sides facing. Pin the folded edges together and machine stitch all round, 3mm from the edge.

12 Pin and tack the ends of the strap to the back and front of the bag and machine stitch down with a rectangle of reinforcing stitches (see page 21).

---

top tip ALTHOUGH YOU DON'T ALWAYS SEE THE LINING FABRIC, THAT DOESN'T MEAN IT HAS GO UNNOTICED. I USED ONE OF MY FLORAL PRINTS INSIDE THIS BAG, IN A COLOURWAY TO MATCH THE CANVAS.

Circles
Laundry Bag

MATERIALS

- 85 x 65cm white linen fabric • scraps of floral print fabric • 2m pink bias binding • 1.2m pink cord
- matching sewing thread • sewing kit • dressmaker's pen or chalk pencil • long ruler or 60cm quilter's rule
- thin card

CUTTING OUT

from white linen fabric • one 82 x 62cm rectangle
from floral print fabric • fifty petals; cut a thin card petal using the template, then for each petal trace the shape on to the wrong side of the fabric and cut out 7mm from outline

This laundry bag is hand appliquéd with a geometric arrangement of petal shapes, a traditional pattern known as 'Hidden Circles'. This is a wonderful way to repurpose tiny pieces of fabric, and the more prints you can find, the more interesting the finished bag will look. I chose a random mixture from my collection – you'll see how a wide range of floral designs always sit happily together even though they vary in scale and colour.

1 Prepare each of the petals for appliqué. Pin the card template centrally on the wrong side of the fabric. Turn back the hem and sew it down through the card with long running stitches. Fold the corners into neat points. Press the turning with a hot iron and when cool, unpick the thread. After a while the card template may become distorted, so make a new one regularly.

2 Position the petals accurately before you stitch them down. You can do this by eye, or by drawing a grid directly on to the fabric. Fold the fabric in half widthways. Press the fold lightly, then unfold.

3 Using a chalk pencil or fading dressmaker's pen, lightly draw a 30 x 40cm rectangle on the right-hand side, 5cm in from the fold, 6cm from the raw right edge, and 6cm up from the bottom edge. Mark three points on the short top and bottom lines at 5cm, 15cm and 25cm from the one corner. Mark four points along the side lines at 5cm, 15cm, 25cm and 35cm from one corner. Join these dots to form a diamond grid.

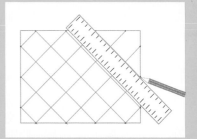

4 Lay 48 of the petals diagonally across the grid, rearranging them until you have a well-balanced layout of pattern and colour. Pin them in place, making sure they all touch at the tips.

top tip CUT OUT EACH OF THE PETALS TIP-TO-TIP ALONG THE DIAGONAL, BIAS GRAIN. THIS PART OF THE FABRIC HAS THE MOST 'GIVE' AND SO THE CURVED EDGES OF THE PETALS WILL LOOK SMOOTH AND CRISP.

Circles
Laundry Bag

5 Slip stitch the petals to the background using small diagonal stitches and a thread that matches the main colour of each fabric.

6 Draw a pencil line 10cm down from the top edge, on the wrong side of the fabric. Bind the top edge and 12cm of each side – to just below the pencil line – with the bias binding.

7 Cut an 84cm length from the remaining binding and press under a 1cm turning at each end. Pin this along the pencil line, so that the neatened ends are aligned with the side edges. Using white sewing thread, machine stitch along the top and bottom edges of the binding, 2mm from the fold.

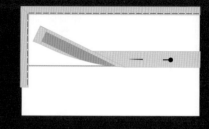

8 Refold the bag widthways and pin the side and bottom edges together. Machine stitch these two edges, leaving a 1cm seam allowance. Start at the bottom corner and end the seam by angling the stitches across the bias binding so that it ends just below the drawstring channel. Neaten the seam allowance with an overlock or zigzag stitch and turn right side out. Press lightly.

10 Tie the ends of the cord together in a loose knot and trim the ends to 10cm. Now it's time to use those two spare petals, to make the tabs. Tack each one over a card template, then leaving the card in place and fold them in half. Starting at the fold, stitch the sides securely together to 5mm from the point. Slip the tab over the end of the cord, securing the point to the cord with a few stitches, then sew the other sides together. Add the other tab in the same way.

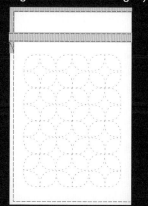

9 Fasten a safety pin to one end of the cord, or thread it through a large bodkin. Feed the cord all the way through the drawstring channel, in one opening and out of the other.

---

top tip AS A FINISHING TOUCH, MY INITIALS WERE EMBROIDERED IN THE BOTTOM LEFT CORNER WITH FINE CHAIN STITCH, WORKED WITH THREE STRANDS OF THREAD. IF YOU ARE MAKING THIS AS A PRESENT YOU COULD ADD YOUR FRIEND'S MONOGRAM OR NAME.

Floral
Washbag

MATERIALS

• 90 x 20cm green floral print fabric • 90 x 20cm pink floral print fabric • 30 x 65cm woven waterproof shower curtain fabric • 25cm white nylon zip • matching sewing thread • sewing kit • sewing machine

CUTTING OUT

from green floral print fabric • twenty 8cm squares
from pink floral print fabric • twenty 8cm squares • two 3 x 5cm zip tabs

One of the most fascinating things about patchwork is the way that you can piece together printed fabrics to create a new design. To make this useful zip-up washbag, squares were cut from two colourways of my Lace Stripe cotton duck and then arranged alternately, which looks as if it has been woven from lengths of floral braid.

1 Lay out the squares for the (identical) front and back, in four rows of five. Alternate the colours and direction of the stripes to create the basketweave effect. Right sides facing, sew the patches together in horizontal rows, leaving a 1cm seam allowance.

2 Press the seam allowances to one side, alternating left and right, as you go down the rows.

3 Hold the top edge of the second row against the bottom edge of the first row together, with the seam matching and the allowances butting up next to each other. Insert a pin at each seam line and the corners, then machine stitch 1cm from the edge. Add the other two rows, then make up the second panel in the same way.

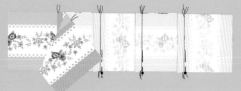

4 Press all the seam allowances open so that the patchwork will lie flat.

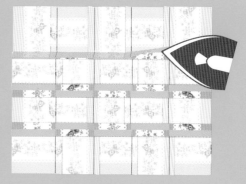

top tip THIS VERSATILE DESIGN CAN BE ADAPTED BY ALTERING THE SIZE OF THE SQUARES:

MAKE THEM SMALLER FOR A MAKE-UP BAG OR LARGER FOR A CHANGING BAG (A GREAT BABY SHOWER GIFT!).

Floral
Washbag

5 Rule a line 2.5cm up from the bottom edge of one panel, and trim along this line. Draw a 2.5cm square at each bottom corner and cut them away. Repeat on the other panel.

6 Pin the panels, wrong sides together, to the waterproof lining. Machine stitch the two layers together, sewing 3mm from the edge of the panels. Cut out neatly.

7 With right sides facing, stitch one of the zip tabs across the tapes at the top end of the zip. Press the seam towards the tab. Lay the zip along the top edge of a bag panel to check the size and sew the other tab to the bottom end, so that the outer edge of

the tab lines up with the side of the bag. (You can stitch through the teeth without damaging the machine needle, as long as you are using a nylon zip, but avoid the tiny metal stopper at the bottom.)

8 Tack the top edge of one side panel to the zip and the tabs with right sides facing. Fit a zip foot to the machine and stitch 6mm from the edge. Sew the other panel to the opposite side, then press the seams lightly and top stitch.

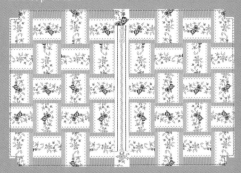

9 Open the zip and fold the bag so that the patchwork lies on the inside. Pin the side and bottom edges together, leaving the squared off corners open. Machine stitch the bottom edge with a 1cm seam, then sew the

top tip IF YOU ARE A REAL PERFECTIONIST, YOU CAN NEATEN THE INSIDE SEAMS WITH AN OVERLOCKING STITCH OR BY BINDING THEM WITH BIAS BINDING, EITHER BY HAND OR MACHINE.

side edges, starting from the corners and sewing towards the zip. Secure both ends of the three seams with reverse stitches. Lightly press them open.

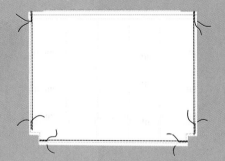

10 Now open out one of the open corners and refold it so that the side seams lines up with the bottom seam. Pin the two edges together and machine stitch with a 6mm seam. Do the same at the other corner, then turn right side out. Ease the corners out to make a flat base for the bag.

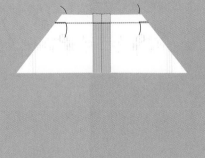

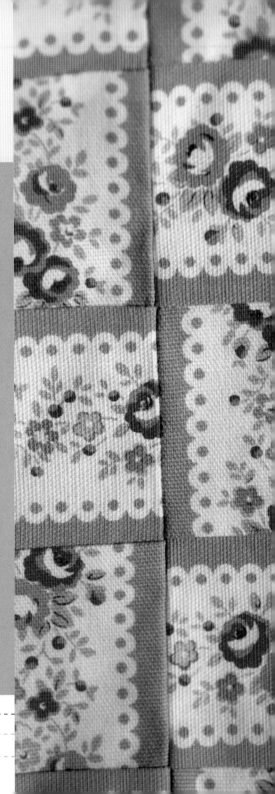

Dresden Plate
Tote Bag

MATERIALS

• 13cm square each of four different floral print fabrics • 13cm square each of red, pink and blue spot print fabrics • 30 x 75cm calico • 90cm of 2cm-wide cotton tape • scrap paper for template • matching sewing thread • sewing kit • sewing machine • 12cm diameter circle template

CUTTING OUT

from floral and red and pink spot print fabrics • six pairs of matching outer petals
from blue spot print fabric • one 12cm circle
from paper • 12 inner petals

This 'Dresden Plate' tote bag is a combination of patchwork, appliqué and hand quilting, and makes a good practical introduction to all three common techniques. This is a very clever way to use up old pieces of fabric as the design options are endless. Here I have used a selection of my signature floral, paisley and mini spot prints, but use whatever you have available at the time. If you like the look of this why not try the 'Dresden Plate' cushion on page 70.

1 Pin a paper template centrally to the wrong side of a petal and fold over the surplus fabric along the two side edges, sewing it down as you go. Don't worry about the raw ends at the point, as they will be concealed by the flower centre. When you come to the curved edge, make a series of little folds to gather in the turning. Tack the fabric down with small stitches and finish off with a double stitch. Cover all the templates in this way.

2 Lay the twelve petals out in a circle and decide on their arrangement – you could sew them together randomly, as shown here, or arrange them so that the matching petals lie opposite each other.

3 Hold the first two petals together with right sides facing. Starting at the right corner, join them with a row of small over stitches, picking up just a couple of threads from the folded fabric on each side. Fasten off at the end, then join the other petals to make the whole flower.

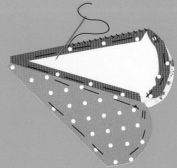

4 Press the flower lightly from the wrong side, then unpick the tacking stitches and remove the templates.

 top tip WHEN YOU ARE TACKING THE FABRIC TO THE PAPER TEMPLATE, START OFF WITH THE KNOT ON THE RIGHT SIDE. THIS WILL MAKE UNPICKING THE THREADS A MUCH QUICKER PROCESS LATER ON.

Dresden Plate
Tote Bag

5 Fold the calico in half widthways. Place the finished flower centrally on the front, about 2cm up from the fold. Pin it in place, through the front layer only.

6 Slip stitch the folded, curved outside edge of the flower to the bag.

7 Now work the quilting that gives the flower its texture and secures it to the bag. Work a line of regularly spaced small stitches about 4mm inside the edge of each petal, starting and ending at the centre.

8 Fold back and tack down a 5mm turning around the edge of the blue spot circle, using a double length of thread. Draw it up tightly to make a Suffolk puff and fasten off the end securely.

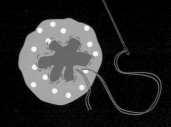

9 Pin the puff to the centre of the flower to completely conceal the raw ends, and slip stitch it into place.

10 Fold the bag in half again, with the right side facing inwards. Pin the two sides together and machine stitch, leaving a 1cm allowance. Neaten the raw edges with an overlocking or zigzag stitch.

11 Press back a 5mm turning around the opening, then turn back and pin down a further 2cm to make a double hem. Machine stitch 3mm down from the top edge and from the fold.

12 Turn the bag so that it is right side out and ease the corners into neat right angles with the point of your embroidery scissors. Press the seams lightly.

13 Cut the tape in half and press under a 5cm turning at each end. Pin the ends of one length to the front of the bag, 6cm in from the corners, so that the folds line up with the lower stitch line. Sew the ends in place with rectangles of machine stitches, reinforced with two diagonal lines worked from corner to corner (see page 21).

14 Make the second handle in the same way and attach to the bag in the corresponding position at the back.

top tip VARIATIONS ON THIS PATTERN PRODUCED SOME OF THE MOST STUNNING PATCHWORK OF THE 1920S AND '30S. IF YOU'VE ENJOYED THIS, WHY NOT THINK ABOUT SEWING A WHOLE QUILT TOP?

Dresden Plate
Cushion

MATERIALS

• *materials as for the bag, plus:* • 35 x 75cm white cotton fabric • safety standard toy or cushion filling

CUTTING OUT
cut all pieces for flower as on page 67
from calico fabric • one 30 x 35cm front panel • two 30 x 20cm back panels
from white cotton fabric • two 32 x 27 rectangles for cushion pad

Here's a variation on a theme – a way to use the skills already learnt whilst making the tote bag. The only extras you'll need are fabric and filling to make a cushion pad.

1 Make the flower as for steps 1–4 on page 67. Centrally pin to the front and hand sew in place. Make the Suffolk puff and stitch it over the raw ends (steps 6–9 on page 68).

2 Press under a 5mm turning on one long edge of a back panel, then press under a second 1cm turning to make a double hem. Machine stitch down. Neaten one long edge of the other panel in the same way.

3 Lay out the front panel with the right side facing upwards. Place one back panel at side edge, with the right sides downwards and the raw edges matching. Pin together all the layers and machine stitch all the way round, leaving a 1cm seam allowance.

4 Turn the cover right side out and clip a small triangle from each corner, cutting to within 3mm of the stitching. Carefully ease out the corners with your embroidery scissors. Press the seams lightly.

5 Cut the tape into four equal lengths and press under a 5mm turning at one end of each. Pin two to the top back panel, 8cm in from the corners, so that the fold lies along the stitched line. Hand stitch in place and snip a small triangle from each loose end.

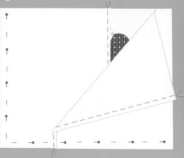

top tip IF YOU DON'T WANT TO MAKE YOUR OWN CUSHION, USE A READY-MADE 30CM SQUARE FEATHER OR POLYESTER PAD, WHICH WILL SQUASH UP TO GIVE THE COVER A WELL-FILLED, UPHOLSTERED APPEARANCE.

Dresden Plate
Cushion

6 Pin the remaining ties to the other back panel, 5cm away from the first two. Hand sew them in place and trim the ends.

7 Pin the two cushion pad panels together. Machine stitch around the outside edge with a 1cm seam allowance, leaving a 10cm gap in one long edge.

8 Press back the seam allowance along the opening then turn right side out. Clip and ease out the corners as for the cover and press the seams. Stuff firmly with the cushion filling, then close the gap with slip stitch. Put the cushion inside the cover and tie two bows at the back.

Rose Linen Pillowcase

MATERIALS

• old printed linen tablecloth • plain linen fabric for back • matching sewing thread • sewing kit • sewing machine

CUTTING OUT

from printed linen fabric • six 28cm squares for front (see step 1)
from linen fabric • one flap: 53 x 20cm • one back panel: 78 x 53cm

I cut the 2 pieces so that the original hem-stitched edge lies along the 53cm sides, meaning ready-finished edges at the opening and I had to adjust the width of the back panel to 76.5cm and the depth of the flap to 18.5cm.

I have a passion for vintage textiles. Even if they show signs of wear, there are usually areas that can be salvaged. When I came across a rose-bordered tablecloth that was in perfect condition apart from a torn centre, I knew it deserved a new lease of life. Here it is transformed into a pretty pillowcase and backed with a linen cut from an old sheet.

1 Draw up a 28cm square template on dressmaker's pattern paper to use as your guide for cutting out the patches. Avoiding any damaged areas, cut one square from each corner of the cloth and two squares from the sides. You can mark guidelines on the template to make sure that the printed design will line up across all six squares.

2 Lay the patches out in their finished order. Starting at the bottom row, pin the side edges of the centre square and one of the corner squares together, with right sides facing. Machine stitch together, leaving a 1.5cm seam allowance. Sew on the other corner square in the same way, then join the three top patches.

3 With right sides facing, place the two pieces together so that the bottom edge of the top row lies against the top row of the bottom row. Line up the seams and pin them at right angles for a precise match. Pin the rest of the seam, and machine stitch 1.5cm from the edge. Press this long seam open.

top tip THE FINISHED SIZE OF THIS CASE IS 50 X 75CM, SO YOU'LL NEED TO ADJUST THE SIZE OF THE SIX PATCHES TO FIT A LARGER OR A LONGER RECTANGULAR PILLOW. FOR A SQUARE PILLOW, CUT FOUR SQUARES, ONE FROM EACH CORNER OF THE ORIGINAL CLOTH.

Rose Linen
Pillowcase

4 If it isn't already neatened, make a narrow double hem along one long edge of the linen flap. Press under 5mm, then a further 1cm turning and top stitch the fold. Hem one short edge of the back panel as necessary.

5 Pin the long raw edge of the flap to one short edge of the finished front. Machine stitch the pieces together, leaving a 1.5cm seam allowance.

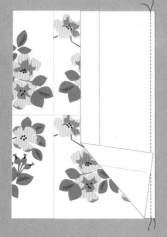

6 Lay the front panel out on your work surface with the right side upwards and open out the flap. Position the back panel over it so that the hemmed edge lies along the seam between the flap and the front panel. Turn the flap over the back panel and pin together along the top, bottom and left side edges.

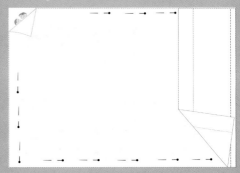

7 Machine stitch the pinned edges, then trim the seam allowance to 6mm. Neaten with a zigzag or overlocking stitch. Turn the pillow case right side out, ease out the corners and press the seams.

top tip THESE HANDLES ARE MADE FROM TORTOISESHELL-LOOK PLASTIC, BUT IF YOU CAN'T FIND ANY SIMILAR, A PAIR OF NATURAL BAMBOO HANDLES WOULD LOOK JUST AS GOOD.

Boudoir Cushion

MATERIALS

• 120 x 60cm curtain lining fabric • scraps of floral print fabric • 8 buttons • matching sewing thread • sewing kit • 25 x 38cm cushion pad

CUTTING OUT

from curtain lining fabric • six 26cm foundation squares • one 27 x 39.5cm back panel
from floral print fabrics • seventeen 7.5cm squares

This sumptuous cushion is made from 'Cathedral Window' patchwork, the technique where sewing meets origami. It first evolved in the 1930s, when it was also known as 'Daisy Block' or 'Mock Orange Blossom'. The folded, petal-shaped frames provide a showcase for tiny fragments of fabric. This uses scraps of lingerie silk and rayon from that era, bordered with a soft sateen lining fabric, for a glamorous look.

1 Start off by creasing the foundation squares into quarters with a cross, as a guideline to help you fold accurately. Fold the side edges together and lightly press the centre crease. Open out, then fold the top and bottom edges together and press the crease. Press a 5mm turning along each edge of the square.

2 With the turnings facing upwards, fold each corner to the centre, so that the edges of the square lie against the guidelines. Press the diagonal folds in turn.

3 Now fold the corner points in once again and press them in place, so a folded square measures 12.5cm by 12.5cm.

4 Make a tiny cross stitch at the centre of the foundation square, through all the layers, to secure the folds and hold down the points.

5 Pin the first two foundation squares together with right sides facing and oversew the top edges together, as for paper-covered patchwork. Join on a third square, then sew the remaining three squares together. Pin both along one long edge, with right sides facing, and oversew. Press the completed piece lightly from the wrong side.

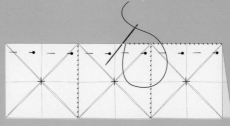

top tip SOME FABRICS I USED IN MY 'WINDOWS' ARE SHEER; I FOUND THE STITCHING BETWEEN THE BLOCKS SHOWED THROUGH.
TO CONCEAL THE JOINS, I POSITIONED 8CM SQUARES OF LEFTOVER LINING FABRIC BEHIND THE FINER SILKS BEFORE FOLDING BACK THE CURVES.

Boudoir Cushion

6 Pin one of the flowered patches to each diamond space between the squares, making sure the colours and patterns are balanced.

7 Turn back and pin down the base squares to conceal the edges of the flowered patches and create shallow curves.

8 Slip stitch down the folded edges through all the layers, using the same colour sewing thread.

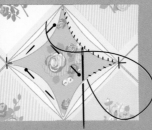

9 To fill in the triangular spaces around the edge, press the remaining patches diagonally in half. Pin them into the gaps and oversew the folds to the outside edges of the foundation squares. Turn back and stitch down the diagonal folds as before to conceal the other two edges.

10 Sew a button to the centre of each of the foundation squares. This not only looks decorative, but will conceal any imperfections in the stitching at the ends of the petals.

11 Make up the cushion by pressing under a 1cm turning all around the back panel. Check that it is the same size as the completed cushion front, adjusting the turnings if necessary, then pin the two together with wrong sides facing. Oversew two long and one short edges, insert the cushion pad, then pin and stitch the opening.

top tip IF YOU ENJOY THIS INTRIGUING TECHNIQUE, WHY NOT GO ON TO MAKE AN ENTIRE QUILT? YOU WON'T HAVE TO BACK OR LINE THE COMPLETED BLOCKS SO IT WILL BE QUICK TO DO, AND BECAUSE IT'S ALL HAND-STITCHED, YOUR WORK WILL BE VERY PORTABLE.

Crazy Patch
Cushion

MATERIALS

• selection of embroidered cloths • 50cm square white linen fabric for cushion front • 40cm square gingham fabric for cushion back • 170cm pink bias binding • 170cm fine piping cord • 40cm square cushion pad • matching sewing thread • 2 skeins pink stranded cotton embroidery thread • sewing kit

Women of past generations spent hours patiently stitching household textiles – tray cloths, napkins and runners – which we seldom use today. Rather than storing these away in a drawer, I wanted to show them off and give them a new lease of life. This crazy patchwork cushion, which uses sections salvaged from a collection of old linens, is my tribute to the work of our grandmothers.

1 Picking out the most interesting areas of embroidery. Cut each patch into a multi-sided shape, with straight edges.

2 Draw a 40cm square in the centre of the white linen cushion front, ruling each line from side to side or top to bottom. Starting in the middle, arrange the patches on the white linen, in a crazy paving style. Overlap the edges to cover the square completely, then pin them in place.

3 Tuck under a 5mm turning along each of the uppermost edges and sew the patches to the linen, with small slip stitches worked in white sewing thread, as close to the folds as possible.

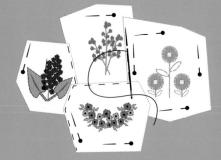

4 Redraw the 40cm square, making sure you go over the edges of the patches where they overlap the outline.

5 Thread a long-eyed needle with three strands of pink embroidery thread and stitch a row of feather stitch (see how to do this on page 29) over each folded edge. Make sure that the outer rows of stitching end 5mm from the pencilled outline.

top tip WASH AND PRESS ALL THE CLOTHS AND DISCARD ANY WORN OR STAINED AREAS. YOU MAY FIND THAT

THE COLOUR OF THE FABRIC MAY VARY FROM SNOW WHITE TO CREAM BUT THIS ONLY ADDS TO ITS CHARM.

Crazy Patch
Cushion

6 Cut the cushion front to size by trimming along the pencil lines. Press back a 1cm turning along each edge. Mitre the corners (see page 21) and tack down the turning.

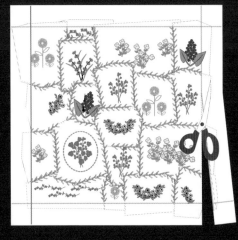

7 Prepare the piping by folding the bias binding over the cord and tacking the two sides together. Fit a zip foot to your sewing machine and sew a line of straight stitch close to the cord (this will keep the piping stable when you hand stitch the cover).

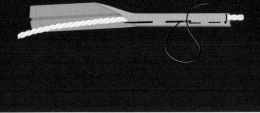

8 Starting close to one corner, pin the piping around the edge of the cover so that the cord peeps over the edge. Hand sew in place with white sewing cotton. Leave the first 3cm unstitched, and make small, closely spaced slip stitches all round the four edges. Fold the ends to the back so that they butt up closely against each other. Sew down on the wrong side and trim to 2cm.

9 Press back 1cm around cushion back, mitring the corners as for the front.

10 Pin the back and front together and slip stitch the cushion back in place around three sides, sewing through the bias binding. Insert the cushion pad, then sew up the final side.

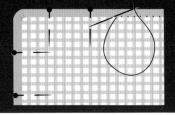

Triangle Patch
Pillowcase

MATERIALS

• a selection of striped and gingham cotton fabrics in reds, blues and white • a man's cotton shirt with button front • 60 x 85cm red and white gingham for backing • matching sewing thread • quilter's ruler • rotary cutter and cutting mat • soft pencil and ruler • sewing kit • sewing machine

To create a crisp, contemporary look, I chose a repeating triangle design that was made up in cotton salvaged from clothing. To save a lot of fiddly stitching, I recycled a shirt front to make the buttoned opening.

1 Wash and press all the fabrics, then cut out eighteen dark and eighteen light 14cm squares. Using a ruler and a sharp, soft pencil, draw a diagonal line across the wrong side of each of the light squares, from corner to corner. Right sides facing, pin together in pairs, one light and one dark. Machine stitch two parallel lines across the square, each one 6mm from the line. Cut the squares apart along the line.

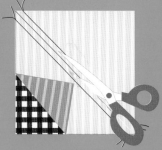

2 Trim the patches to 11.5cm square, then press all the seam allowances towards the darker patches. Lay them out in five horizontal rows of 7 squares, with the dark triangles pointing towards the bottom right corner. Take time to rearrange them until the colours and patterns are evenly balanced.

3 Join the squares in vertical rows of five, starting at the top left corner. Pin the first two patches together with right sides facing, so that the bottom edge of the first square lies along the top edge of the second one. Machine stitch, leaving a seam allowance of 6mm, then join on the other three patches in the same way. Double check that all the dark triangles are facing in the same direction, as it's very easy to get them the wrong way round at this stage!

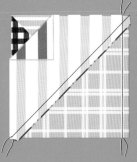

4 When the row is complete, press all the straight seam allowances towards the first square. Repeat with the other 6 rows.

top tip THE PILLOWSLIP IS QUICKLY ASSEMBLED USING A ROTARY CUTTER AND QUILTER'S RULER TO MAKE THE 'HALF SQUARE TRIANGLE' PATCHES. LEARN HOW TO USE A ROTARY CUTTER ON PAGE 17.

Triangle Patch
Pillowcase

5 Now join the rows together. With right sides facing, hold the left edge of the first row against the right edge of the second row, matching the seams exactly. Insert a pin at each seam line and at both corners.

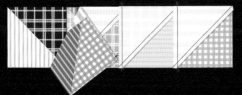

6 Machine stitch 6mm from the edge, then add the other five rows. Press all the seams in the same direction, towards the right.

7 Cut a rectangle of gingham to exactly the same width as the completed patchwork (approximately 53cm), but 5.5cm longer. This will be the back of the pillowslip.

8 Trim the buttonhole and button bands from one of the shirts. Each strip should be 6cm wide and as long as possible.

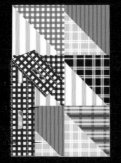

9 With right sides facing, pin the buttonhole strip to the left edge of the patchwork front and machine stitch with a 6mm seam allowance. Neaten the seam with a zigzag or overlocking stitch and press away from the buttonholes.

10 Pin the button band to the back, in the same way. Check that the buttons will line up exactly with the buttonholes, then sew in place and neaten the seam.

11 Fold the button band to the wrong side of the back along the seam line, then with right sides facing pin the top front and back together. Machine stitch 6mm from the edge around three sides and neaten the seam. Turn right side out, ease out the corners and press the side seams.

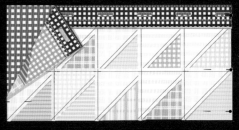

top tip TO MAKE THE BUTTON BAND LOOK A BIT MORE INTERESTING, I SNIPPED OFF THE ORIGINAL BUTTONS AND
SEWED ON A MULTI-COLOURED SELECTION SAVED FROM THE OTHER SHIRTS I HAD COLLECTED.

Suffolk Puff
Cushion

MATERIALS

• 120 x 55cm red spot print fabric • 120 x 25cm blue spot print fabric • about 120 x 25cm in floral prints with a white background • 94 x 42cm plain blue cotton fabric • tea bags • washing-up bowl • wooden spoon • matching sewing thread • sewing machine • sewing kit • 40cm square cushion pad

CUTTING OUT

from red spot print fabric • 45 circles
from blue spot print fabric • 16 circles
from other print fabrics • 20 circles

When I discovered a square of Suffolk Puff patchwork amidst a bundle of vintage textiles I decided the pretty, softly faded fabrics needed a second chance. The panel was stitched to the front of a plain pink cushion and I was delighted with the way the unexpectedly bright colour peeped out through the spaces between the puffs. This inspired me to create a cushion cover from my own spot, star and floral haberdashery fabrics, but to keep the softness of the original piece I first dipped all the fabric in strong tea to tone down the colours.

1 Launder any new fabrics to remove the dressing used in the manufacturing process. Make up a dye bath by steeping five tea bags (traditional strong English breakfast tea rather anything fruity or herbal!) in a washing-up bowl of very hot water. Remove them after about fifteen minutes.

2 Add the fabrics and leave them to soak for thirty minutes, stirring them with a wooden spoon now and again to ensure even coverage. Rinse, then leave to dry naturally and press well. Remember that the fabric will dry to a lighter shade, so if you would like it to be darker, just go through the whole process again.

3 Trace an 11cm diameter template on to paper and use this as a guide to cut out the fabric circles, as listed above.

4 Thread a long needle with a long length of thread and knot the ends together so that it is double.

5 To make a circle of fabric into a puff, fold back a 5mm turning around the circumference and stitch it down with a round of evenly spaced running stitches. The smaller the stitches, the finer your gathers will be: the ones used for the cushion shown here were 8mm long with equal gaps between them.

top tip SUFFOLK PUFFS CAN BE STITCHED TOGETHER IN MANY DIFFERENT WAYS: TRY ARRANGING THEM IN STRAIGHT ROWS, A CHEQUERBOARD PATTERN, DIAGONAL LINES OR JUST HAPHAZARDLY FOR A LESS FORMAL LOOK.

91

Suffolk Puff Cushion

6 Gently draw up the thread to gather the circle, using the tip of your needle to push the raw edges inside if necessary. Take the needle down through the finished puff and fasten off the thread securely on the wrong side with a few short back stitches. Trim the thread close to the surface.

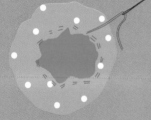

7 Arrange the finished puffs in nine rows of nine, with the red spot ones around the outside edge and forming a central cross. Each corner then has five white and four blue spot puffs.

8 Sew together the top row of puffs. Hold the first two together with right sides facing and make several small, tight overstitches to join the edges together. Take the needle to the opposite side of the puff and sew on the next one in the same way. Do the same all the way along the row, making sure that the stitches all lie in a straight line, then fasten off securely. Join the other eight rows in the same way and lay them back out the the right order.

9 Now comes the tricky bit: joining the rows. Start by holding the top two rows together with right sides facing. Join the first puff of each row with a few stitches, then take the needle across to the bottom edge of the second row. Sew this point to the first puff of the third row, then repeat the process so that all the first puffs are stitched together.

top tip IF YOU'RE NOT A TEA DRINKER, DON'T WORRY. STRONG, FRESHLY BREWED COFFEE CAN ALSO BE USED TO CHANGE THE COLOUR OF YOUR FABRIC, AND WILL GIVE IT A WARMER, BROWNER TONE.

10 Join all the second puffs, then the third, and continue until the cover is completed. Check for any weak joins and re-stitch.

11 Turn under and press a 1cm double hem at each short end of the blue rectangle.

12 Place the fabric face upwards on your work surface and turn back 25cm at each edge. Pin the top and bottom edges together through all the layers and machine stitch, leaving a 1cm seam allowance.

13 Turn the cover right side out and press. Place it face down on the finished puff cushion front, adjusting the position so that half a circle projects at each edge. Pin the cover to the cushion front and slip stitch the two together around the edge of the cover. Insert the cushion pad.

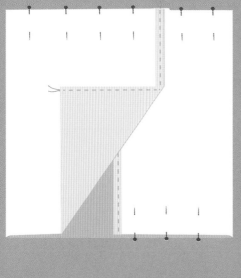

Child's Cushion

MATERIALS

a minimum of • 60 x 40cm check fabric • 40 x 10cm small-scale floral fabric • 40 x 10cm large-scale floral fabric • old envelopes and paper • matching sewing thread • sewing machine • sewing kit • 25cm cushion pad

TEMPLATES

from check fabric • one 10cm square • two 16 x 26cm back panels
from small-scale floral print fabric • four 10cm squares
from large-scale floral print fabric • four 10cm squares
from paper • nine 8cm square templates

This simple cushion cover, made from nine bright squares, pays homage to one of the first sewing projects I did as a little girl. I can vividly remember sitting patiently as I completed each fabric-covered template in turn, and then the huge sense of achievement when I learnt how to stitch them together. It would still be a perfect starting point for beginners or for any newcomers to English-style patchwork.

1 Thread your needle and keep it ready to hand. Pin a paper square centrally to the back of one of the fabric squares so that there is a 1cm margin all round.

2 Fold the top margin back over the template. Starting with the knot on the right side, sew the fabric to the paper with long running stitches. Fold over the next margin so that you have a neat right angle at the

corner. Tack down this edge, then stitch down the other two edges. Work a double stitch to secure the thread and trim the end to 2cm. Cover all the papers in the same way.

3 Using the photograph opposite as your guide, lay the squares out in three rows of three, with the check patch in the centre surrounded by the eight flowery patches.

4 Pick up the first two squares on the top row. With the fabric sides facing, hold them together so that the left edge of the second square lies along the right edge of the first square.(Don't worry, this will make sense when you do it!)

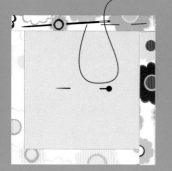

Child's Cushion

5 Starting at the right hand corner, sew the two patches together using some small overcast stitches.

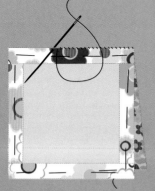

6 Join the third square to complete the row, then make up the other two rows.

7 Now it's time to sew the three rows together in just the same way, making sure that the seam lines match up as you go. When you get to the end of the thread, make three stitches in the opposite direction to secure the end of the seam and trim the tail to 5mm.

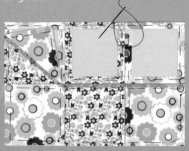

8 Then you have finished sewing, unpick and remove all the papers, then open out the turnings around the outside edge. Press these so that they lie flat.

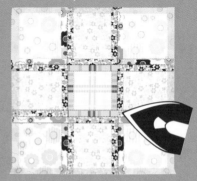

9 Press under a 1cm double turning along one long edge of each back panel. Sew this down by hand or machine.

10 Place the cushion front on your work surface with the right side facing upwards. Position one back panel, face downwards, on the left of the cushion front so that the raw edges are matching. Lay the other panel on the right, then pin the layers together around all four sides.

12 Snip a tiny triangle from each corner, 5mm from the stitching. Turn it right side out and ease out the corners into sharp angles with a pencil. Press the seams lightly then insert the cushion pad.

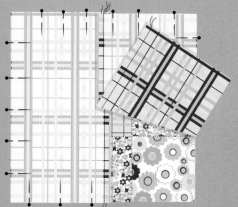

11 Machine stitch all the way around the edge of the cushion cover, leaving a 1cm seam allowance.

top tip MAKE THIS CUSHION INTO A SOUVENIR OF CHILDHOOD BY USING SCRAPS OF FABRIC FROM OUTGROWN SHIRTS, BLOUSES AND DRESSES. THEN SEW ON A FEW BUTTONS OR EMBROIDERED MOTIFS FROM THE GARMENTS AS EXTRA DECORATION.

MATERIALS

• twelve scraps of cotton, at least 15cm square • used envelopes or old letters • tacking thread • matching sewing thread • 250g polyester toy stuffing • sewing kit

Every budding sports star has to start somewhere, so this soft patchwork ball is guaranteed to provide hours of goal practice. It's made from twelve hand-stitched pentagons – a variation on the usual honeycomb hexagon technique – and the pictorial fabrics are a blend of vintage nursery finds and my own prints for children.

1 Trace or photocopy the full-size pentagon. Using this as your guide, cut out twelve pentagons from recycled paper.

2 Pin a paper pentagon to the wrong side of the first fabric scrap, centring it over either a motif or an interesting pattern area. Cut the fabric to the same pentagon shape but adding a margin, snipping approximately 1cm from the edges of the paper. Fold the fabric margin over each side of the paper pentagon in turn, stitching it to the paper as you go.

3 The ball is made in two separate halves. When you have covered all the papers, plan the layout for both parts. Choose the two strongest motifs and arrange five patches around each one, balancing the colours evenly on each side.

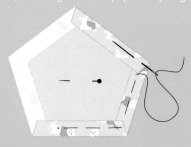

top tip THE FINISHED BALL MEASURES ABOUT 15CM IN DIAMETER, BUT YOU CAN CHANGE THE SIZE OF THE TEMPLATE TO MAKE IT LARGER OR SMALLER: 2.5CM PENTAGONS WOULD MAKE A TINY BALL THAT YOU COULD USE FOR A CHRISTMAS DECORATION.

Child's
Pentagon Ball

4 Pick out the centre pentagon and one from the edge, and hold them together with right sides facing. Bring a threaded needle out through the right corner of the front patch, then oversew them along one edge. Work a few extra stitches at each end of the row to reinforce the seam.

6 Seam the two halves together, remembering to reinforce all corners. At this stage the ball can be a bit awkward to hold, so fold it whichever way feels comfortable for you and adjust the two parts as you sew each pair of sides together. Leave the last two edges unstitched.

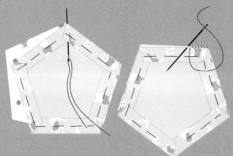

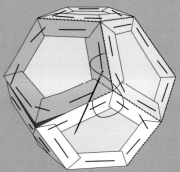

5 Sew the third patch to the next edge of the centre pentagon in the same way. To join the second and third patches, fold the centre patch in half so that the other two face each other and stitch the two adjacent edges together. Join on the remaining three patches in the same way, then make up the second half of the ball.

7 Unpick all the paper pentagons and remove. Turn the ball right side out through the gap and stuff with wadding. Carry on filling it until the ball has a good round shape, then oversew the gap to close.

top tip CHOOSE A POLYESTER TOY FILLING THAT MEETS SAFETY STANDARDS AND USE THE HANDLE OF A WOODEN SPOON TO PACK IT
DOWN. REMEMBER THAT TO MAKE A GOOD, SOLID BALL IT MAY TAKE MORE STUFFING THAN YOU EXPECT.

Stanley Toy

As you may have guessed, this is one of my favourite projects, a patchwork of my dog Stanley. I have to admit that he's almost as adorable as the original! He's made from a mix of fabrics in reds and blues, in dots, flowers, cowboys and Mini Stanley.

The seam allowance throughout is 6mm.

1 Stanley is made from two dog-shaped side panels which are joined with a gusset loop. Lay out 35 squares and 5 triangles to make the left-facing side panel. Right sides facing, pin and stitch the patches in horizontal rows.

2 Iron the seam allowances on the top row to the left, then press the seams on the next row to the right. Press all the other rows, alternating the direction in which they lie. The muzzle goes to the right, as does the top two legs. The bottom leg lies on the left.

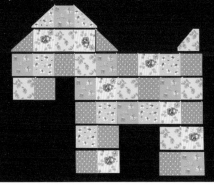

3 To assemble the body, pin the bottom edge of the top head row to the top edge of the next row down, matching up the seams. Machine stitch. Press this and all the other horizontal seams downwards.

4 Join the head to the top row of the body. Add the muzzle, other two body rows, two legs and tail. Make up the right-facing body panel the same way, reversing the direction.

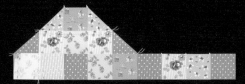

5 With right sides facing, pin the ears together in pairs and sew around the curved edges. Trim the seam back to 3mm at the tips. Turn right side out, and press. Tack in place at the top of the head.

6 The gusset is a mixture of squares and rectangles. The rectangles lie next to the triangular patches at head and tail, and the squares next to the other body squares. Each of the 16 straight edges are assembled separately, then joined to make a loop.

top tip

MATERIALS

• dress-weight cotton in mixed prints • scrap of black felt or leather • 7 litres of polyester toy filling • two 2cm black buttons • sewing machine • sewing kit

CUTTING OUT

from mixed print fabrics • one hundred 7cm squares • ten triangles • five 7 x 10cm rectangles
from red spot fabric • four ears
from felt or leather • one nose

7 Start at the tail and join six squares for Stan's back end. Seam two squares for the back paw, two squares for the inside leg, two squares for Stan's underbelly, and so on until you reach the tip of his nose. Seam two rectangles for his forehead, pick a single patch for the crown, two rectangles for the back of his head, three squares for his back and the final rectangle for his tail. Press the seams in one direction. Lay all the pieces in place around the left-facing body panel.

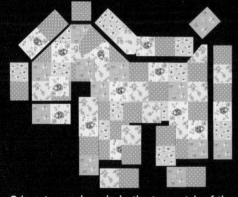

8 Insert a marker pin in the top patch of the first strip so you can find it again. With right sides facing, pin the top of the sole strip to the bottom end. Sew together, leaving 6mm unstitched at each end of the seam. Join the rest of the strips and single patches in the same way, then join to make a loop. Press the seams open.

9 Starting at the tail tip, pin the loop to the body with right sides facing. Fold out the open ends of the seams so that the gusset will fit neatly. Sew all the way round, 6mm from the edge. Repeat with the right-facing panel, leaving the underbelly unstitched.

10 Turn right side out and push out the corners. Pack the toy filling into the paws, muzzle and tail, then the head and body and push down firmly. Slip stitch the opening with a double length of thread.

11 Sew the eyes to the sides of the head and stitch the nose with tiny overcast stitches.

12 Make a collar from a 35 x 10cm strip of red cotton fabric. Press in half widthways, then press under a 1cm turning at both long edges. Refold and top stitch 3mm from each edge. Fold under the edges and fit around Stan's neck. Trim the ends to fit snugly, then sew them together.

top tip AS A FINISHING TOUCH I HAD A BONE-SHAPED DOG TAG ENGRAVED WITH STAN'S NAME AND ATTACHED IT TO THE FABRIC COLLAR. YOUR LOCAL KEY-CUTTER SHOULD HAVE SOMETHING SIMILAR.

Bunny
Blanket

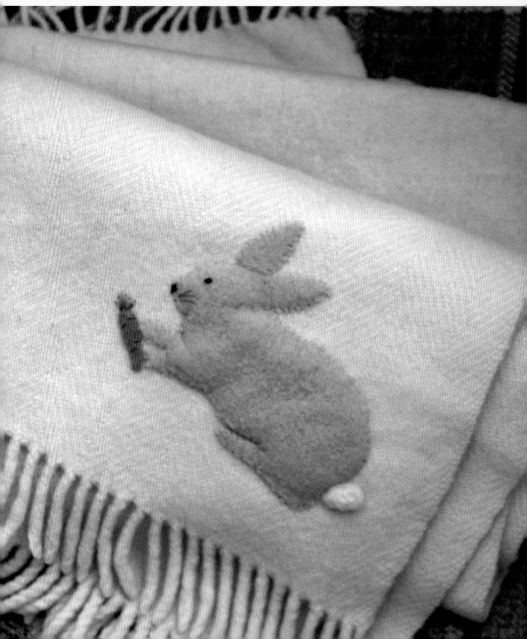

MATERIALS

• 45cm square 10-count canvas • tapestry frame • fringed cream blanket • 15 x 13cm blue felt • matching sewing thread • scrap of orange felt • small amount of polyester toy filling • stranded embroidery thread in green and black • tracing paper and pencil • sewing kit

I like this adorable rabbit patch so much that I have used it twice, adapting it in two quite different ways. Here it is cut from blue felted wool, gently padded and appliquéd to the corner of a vintage cream blanket. Have a look at the other version on page 148 – a flowery bunny would look equally good.

1 Photocopy the bunny template and cut out around the outside edge. Pin to the blue felt, then cut out close to the paper.

2 Pin the bunny to the corner of the blanket. Sew it down by hand with tiny over stitches, leaving 3cm open in the centre of the back.

3 Stuff small amounts of polyester filling through this space, using a pencil to push them right into the head, paws and tail end, then sew up the gap.

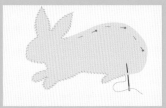

4 Embroider the eyes and nose in satin stitch (see page 28), using a single thread of black embroidery cotton. Add a few short black straight stitches to act as the bunny's whiskers.

5 Using blue thread, work curved rows of small running stitches at the front and back legs as indicated on the template. Cut out a little carrot from orange felt and sew it down around the edge with matching thread. Add a tuft of long, thin green chain stitches or several straight stitches to the top of the carrot (see page 29).

6 To make the tail, carefully snip off one strand of the fringe from the outside edge of the blanket (preferably on the opposite side to the bunny). Curl it up into an oval and stab stitch securely in place.

top tip THE RAISED TAIL AND WOOLLEN FRINGE MEAN THAT THIS TYPE OF DECORATED BLANKET SHOULD BE GIVEN ONLY TO OLDER CHILDREN (AS THERE MAY BE A CHOKING HAZARD FOR SMALL BABIES).

Star
Throw

MATERIALS

for each block • 45cm square of white cotton • 20 x 20cm of 4 print fabrics • 10cm square dark fabric • 10cm square fusible bonding web • print fabric for binding • matching sewing thread • sewing kit • sewing machine

CUTTING OUT

for each star • eight star points, two from each fabric
for the binding • one 8cm wide strip, 10cm longer than the sum of all four sides (join strips to required length)

MEASURING UP

twenty blocks set in 4 rows of 5 = 178 x 221cm: adapt these proportions to suit your own bed

An ideal bedcover for sunny summer days, this throw is a contemporary re-working of a classic design. It consists of just a single layer of fabric, bound at the edge and decorated with a pattern of patchwork stars. These are a variation on the 'Dresden Plate' pattern and because each star is stitched to an individual square block the finished size can be as large or small as you wish.

1 Mark 2 dots at the two top corners on the seam line on each of the star point patches.

2 Arrange eight patches in their finished star shape. With right sides facing, pin the first two together along one long edge. Machine stitch as far as the dot, then work a few backwards stitches to secure the seam and trim the thread. Add the other six patches in this way, then join the first and last together to complete the star.

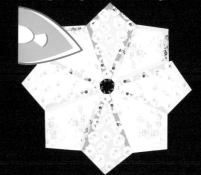

3 Press all the seams open and press back a 6mm turning along each outer edge.

4 Neaten the edge of the white square with an overlocking or zigzag stitch. Press it very lightly in half, then half again to mark it into quarters. Pin the finished star to the square, lining the points up with the crease lines. Sew in place, either by hand or with a narrow machine buttonhole or zigzag stitch.

 THE STARS ON MY THROW ARE ALL IDENTICAL, BUT THIS DESIGN LOOKS EQUALLY EFFECTIVE WHEN EACH SQUARE HAS A DIFFERENT STAR MADE FROM EIGHT RANDOMLY SELECTED PRINTS.

Star
Throw

5 Trace the octagon template on to the paper side of the bonding web. Iron to the back of the dark fabric and cut out around the outline. Peel off the backing and position in the centre of the star. Press and machine stitch around the edge in a matching thread. Repeat with the remaining squares.

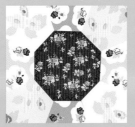

6 Lay out all your finished squares. With right sides facing, join them in horizontal rows with a 1cm seam. Press all the seams open.

7 Again with right sides facing, pin the bottom edge of the top row to the top edge of the second row, matching the seams exactly. Machine stitch and press the seam open. Add the other rows in the same way.

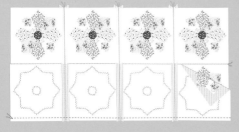

8 Press under a 1cm turning one long edge of the binding strip. With right sides facing and raw edges matching, pin it along the top edge of the throw, trimming the ends in line with the fabric. Machine stitch, then turn the folded edge over to the back. Pin it down so that the fold lies 3mm beyond the stitch line. Machine stitch in place from the front, sewing along the seam line between the throw and the binding. Bind the bottom edge in the same way.

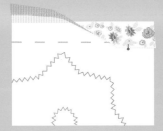

9 When binding the side edges, fold under 1cm at each end of the fabric strip, and pin it down so that the folds project 1mm beyond the edges. Machine stitch and fold over as before, then stitch down from the front. Slip stitch the edges of the folds.

top tip USE AN OLD WHITE SHEET – COTTON OR LINEN – FOR THE BACKING
SQUARES AS AN ECO-ALTERNATIVE TO BUYING NEW FABRIC.

Hankie
Bedcover

MATERIALS
• printed hankies • flat sheet to fit finished cover • matching sewing thread • sewing machine • sewing kit

HOW MANY HANKIES?
The hankies are 50cm square. You will need 3 rows of 5 for a single bed, 4 rows of 5 for a double, 5 rows of 5 for a king size and as many as 6 rows of 5 for a super king. Measure up your bed first and decide how much of an overhang you would like at each side, then round off to the nearest 50cm.

The Stone Roses hankie is far too pretty to be hidden away in a handbag or tucked away in a pocket. The design is an adaptation of one of my fabrics, with a deep curved border of blooms set around a central spray, and it is just one of a series of printed handkerchiefs. I love the way that new shapes are created when the pattern is repeated, but the same technique would work equally well with an assortment of different designs.

1 Prepare the hankies by removing the labels, then laundering and pressing them. Wash and iron the backing sheet too if it's a new one, then there's no possibility of shrinkage in the future.

2 Join them first in short rows of three or more. Pin together with right sides facing and machine stitch 1cm from the hem. Press the seams open.

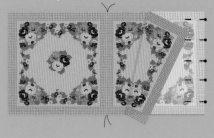

3 Lay the first two rows together along one long edge, with right sides facing, and line up the seams. Insert a pin through each point that they meet, then pin the rest of the edges. Stitch and press as before, and continue until you have joined all the rows.

4 You'll need plenty of space for this step, so make sure you have a nice clean floor! Spread out and smooth the sheet. Place the hankies face down on top, lining the two up along one side and the bottom edge. Pin them together with the pins parallel to the hems, and trim the sheet to the same size as the hankies.

5 Machine stitch all the way round, leaving a 1cm seam allowance. Leave a 50cm gap along one edge and turn the cover right side out through this opening. Press back a 1cm turning along each side of the opening, pin the two layers and slip stitch to close.

top tip I KNOW THAT IT'S NOT REALLY A PATCH PROJECT, BUT A SINGLE HANDKERCHIEF MAKES A GREAT CUSHION COVER! IMAGINE A WHOLE ROW OF THEM, EACH ONE IN A DIFFERENT FLORAL OR GREETINGS PRINT.

Curtain
Panel

MATERIALS

• floral fabric • striped fabric for the sashing, plus extra for the header and facing • plain fabric for little sashing squares • 10cm curtain header tape the same width as finished curtain • curtain hooks • matching sewing thread • sewing machine • sewing kit

Like some of the best patchwork, this curtain is a combination of old and new fabrics. Large patches cut from my extravagant Blooms furnishing print are sashed with strips of vintage flannel shirting and offset with small squares of plain red cotton.

HOW MUCH FABRIC?

First measure up to find the finished size of your curtain. The drop or length will be the distance between the bottom of your curtain pole and the window sill or floor. The width will be one and a half times the length of the pole for a single panel, or one and a half times half the width for each curtain of a pair.

For the curtain you will need 12cm of 136cm wide plain, 35cm of 136cm wide striped and at least 50cm of 148cm wide floral fabric for each finished square metre (or even more if you want to include a lot of very flowery patches).

For the facings you'll need enough striped fabric to make two 8cm strips the same length as the curtain, one 8cm strip the same width and one 12cm strip the same width. You can join the fabric as necessary to create the right length.

CUTTING OUT

Cut the plain fabric into 8cm squares and the striped into eight 20cm rectangles with the stripe running lengthways. Cut the floral print into 20 cm squares, selecting different areas of the repeat for each one. Approximately 1 square metre of patchwork requires 16 large squares, 32 rectangular sashing strips and 16 small squares.

top tip IF YOU ARE MAKING A CURTAIN AS LARGE AS MINE, TRY TO PIECE IT ALL IN A SINGLE SESSION, OR LEAVE THE PATCHES LAID OUT IN A PLACE WHERE THE LAYOUT WON'T BE DISTURBED.

Curtain Panel

1 Lay all the large squares out and shuffle them around so that the more densely patterned ones are at the centre and there is a border of leaves and sprigs. Add in the squares and rectangles that make up the sashing. You will need sashing rows at the side and bottom edges to frame the panel, but not at the top edge.

2 Start by sewing together the horizontal rows of squares and rectangles in pairs. Pin the short ends of each patch together with right sides facing, then machine stitch leaving a 1cm seam allowance. You can speed up the process by chain piecing and then snipping them apart.

3 Join these pairs together, with right sides facing and a 1cm seam. Sew the final square of each row to the end of the last rectangle.

4 Press the seam allowances so that they lie towards the rectangles.

5 Join the vertical rectangles to the large squares, in horizontal rows, with a 1cm seam. Start at the left of each row and join a patch at a time. Sew the last rectangle in each to the right edge of the final square.

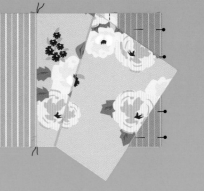

top tip WHEN CUTTING OUT FABRIC WITH A WOVEN (NOT PRINTED) STRIPE, CUT IT FIRST INTO A LONG STRIP, FOLLOWING THE STRIPES, THEN USE A ROTARY CUTTER AND RULER TO TRIM IT INTO RECTANGLES.

6 When each row is complete, press the seam allowances towards the rectangles.

7 Starting at the bottom, sew the patches and sashing together. Place the first two rows together with right sides facing, so that the top edge of the sashing lies along the bottom edge of the patches. Insert a pin through both seams at the points where they meet. Pin the corners and the spaces between the pins, then machine stitch with a 1cm seam allowance. Press the seam towards the sashing. Join all the rows in this way.

Curtain Panel

8 Cut an 8cm strip of striped fabric to fit along the bottom edge to make the facing. Press under a 6mm turning along one long edge. Pin the raw edge to the curtain with right sides facing and machine stitch with a 1cm seam. Turn the facing to the wrong side, pin and tack down the turning and machine stitch from the right side, close to the long seam line. Press.

9 Neaten the two side edges in the same way. Cut the facings so that they are 2cm longer than the curtains and sew them on so that this extra fabric extends below the bottom edge. Press it under, in line with the hem, before folding back and sewing down the facings.

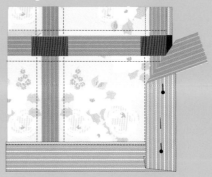

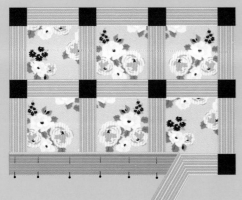

top tip THIS PANEL IS UNLINED, SO THE VARIOUS MATERIALS TAKE ON A WONDERFUL STAINED GLASS-LIKE QUALITY WHEN HUNG AGAINST A SUNLIT WINDOW.

10 Cut a 12cm strip to go along the curtain header (or top edge), adding an extra 4cm. Press back a 3cm turning along one long edge. Pin the raw edge to the curtain with right sides facing, so that 2cm extends at each end. Machine stitch 1cm from the edge and press the seam up towards the facing.

12 Press under 1cm at each end of the header tape. Draw out the three gathering cords at at both ends, then pin and stitch the tape to the top of the curtain, so that the top edge lies 2cm down from the fold and the bottom edge conceals the seam.

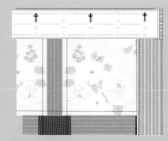

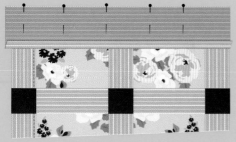

11 Press back the extra fabric so that it is in line with the side edges.

13 Gather the cords to the required width and knot. Insert the curtain hooks and hang in place.

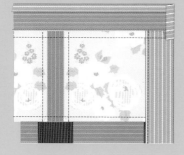

Tea Towel
Tablecloth

MATERIALS
• linen and cotton tea towels • large reel of sewing thread • sewing kit • sewing machine

MEASURING UP
An average tea towel is 40 x 60cm. Instead of getting into any complicated calculations, the best way to work out how many you will need is to gather together all your old tea towels and lay them over the tabletop, allowing a 50cm overhang at each edge!

When I had a look through my linen cupboard to find a suitable cloth for my new dining table I couldn't find anything that was the right size. However, the neatly folded stacks of linen tea towels, with their unexpected combinations of stripes and checks, gave me an idea... here are the biggest patches in the book!

1 Pick out the smallest tea towel and cut away the hemmed edges and any selvedges. You can do this by following the woven stripes or by drawing guidelines with a fabric marker and a large quilting rule.

2 Trim all the other towels down to the same size, using the small towel as a template. Pin it to each one in turn, centering it over the design, and cut away the margins.

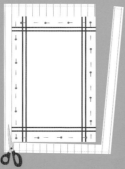

3 Neaten the edge of each by machine with a wide zigzag or an overlocking stitch. This will take a while, but it's worth it in the end!

4 Clear the floor and lay out the towels in rows. As with any other patchwork, you should aim for a good balance of colour and pattern, so take time to shuffle them about until you are pleased with the arrangement.

5 Join the horizontal rows along the long edges with a 1.5cm seam. Press all the seams open (this makes the cloth flatter than if they are pressed to one side).

6 Pin the first two rows together along one long edge, matching the seams and corners exactly. Join with a 1.5cm seam and press the seam open. Repeat with the other rows.

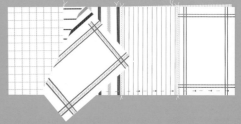

7 Press under a 1.5cm turning around the outside edge of the finished cloth. Mitre each of the corners (see page 21), then pin and machine down the hem 12mm from the fold.

top tip USE A MIXTURE OF OLD AND NEW TEA TOWELS, BUT WASH THEM ALL ON A HOT SETTING AND PRESS WELL BEFORE STITCHING: THEY MIGHT SHRINK AT DIFFERENT RATES WHICH MAY DISTORT YOUR FINISHED CLOTH.

Sugarbag Doorstop

MATERIALS

• scraps of printed canvas or furnishing weight fabric • 18cm of 2.5cm-wide webbing • 20cm of 2cm-wide velcro plastic beads or 2kg rice for filling • matching sewing thread • sewing kit • sewing machine

CUTTING OUT

from print fabric • twenty-seven 6 x 10cm rectangles • ten 6cm squares
from plain fabric • two 11 x 18cm rectangles for base

A doorstop is one of those indispensable home accessories, but there's no reason why it shouldn't be decorative. My patchwork version, in shades of dusky pink, olive and chocolate brown, combines large polka dots with furnishing size roses and a tiny floral sprig. It shows just how effective a mixture of fabric with different scale prints can look if you restrict yourself to a limited palette.

The seam allowance is 1cm throughout. Press each seam open after stitching.

1 All four side panels are made in the same way, from five rectangles and two squares. Lay out the patches for the first side as in the drawing. Starting at the bottom, join the two rectangles together. Next, go to the top left and sew the two squares to the adjacent horizontal rectangles. Join these two pieces together horizontally, then add the vertical rectangle to the right edge. Add the two joined rectangles to the bottom edge.

2 Draw a point 1cm in from the top and bottom edges at each corner, to mark the ends of the seam lines.

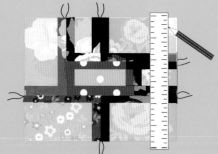

3 With right sides facing, pin two panels together along one side edge, making sure that they are both the same way up and the seams and corners are aligned. Machine stitch between the dots so that 1cm remains open at each end of the seam. Add the other two panels, then join the remaining sides.

top tip IF YOU ARE USING RICE AS A FILLING, LINE THE DOORSTOP WITH A LARGE PLASTIC BAG FIRST AND SEAL IT WITH PARCEL TAPE. THIS WAY IT WILL STAY DRY AND THERE'S NO DANGER OF MOULD OR MILDEW.

Sugarbag Doorstop

4 The top panel is made from the remaining two squares and seven rectangles, laid out as shown below. Firstly sew the two horizontal rectangles at the bottom together and add a vertical rectangle at each side. Join the two squares to the adjacent rectangles and then sew these two pieces. Add the vertical rectangle to the right edge, then sew the two halves together.

5 Mark the ends of the seams on the wrong side, as for the side panels.

6 Pin the two ends of the webbing centrally to the sides of the top panel. Machine stitch 5mm from the edge, working two or three rows backwards and forwards to reinforce.

7 With the right side facing downwards pin one edge of the top panel to the top edge of one of the joined side panels. Machine stitch between the dots, working a few backwards stitches to reinforce both ends of the seam. Sew the other three edges in the same way.

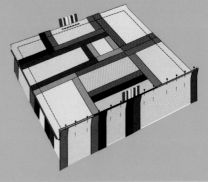

8 Press a 1cm turning over to the right side of one long edge of a base panel. Pin the fuzzy side of the velcro over the turning so that the right edge lies along the fold and machine stitch in place. Press the turning on the other panel to the wrong side and sew the hooked velcro over the turning in the same way.

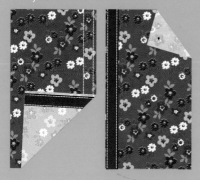

9 Mark the ends of the seams on the outer corners as for the side panels. Stick the two pieces together, making sure that the top and bottom edges measure 18cm. Sew to the base of the doorstop in the same way as the top panel.

10 Trim a triangle 5mm from each corner seam to reduce bulk at the corners.

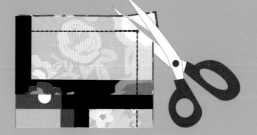

11 Open up the velcro and turn the door stop right side out. Ease out the seams and corners, then fill with the rice or beads (using a large serving spoon is the least messy way to do this) and close the velcro once again.

Tartan
Beanbag

MATERIALS

• a minimum of 1m x 50cm each of three plaid fabrics • 80 x 70cm plaid for base • 0.5 sq m safety standard polystyrene beads in liner • 54cm velcro • dressmaker's squared paper • matching sewing thread • sewing machine • sewing kit

CUTTING OUT

from three plaid fabrics • Cut the fabrics into 15cm strips, following the woven lines to keep the edges straight. Snip the strips into patches of different widths, ranging from 8 to 20cm wide.
from base plaid fabric • Fold the template along the line. Use the larger side as a guide to cut 2 base panels.

Patchwork isn't all about ditsy floral prints. Larger scale geometrics have a striking, bolder look and I really like the somewhat haphazard effect you get by juxtaposing plaids, tartans and checks. This squashy beanbag is covered in a combination of three woven fabrics, which started out as cotton picnic blankets. It would make versatile extra seating or footstool, but it's so comfortable that it might just be commandeered by the family pet.

The seam allowance is 1.5cm throughout. Press each seam open after stitching.

1 Make a circle template by drawing onto dressmaker's paper a circle with a 62cm diameter. Draw on a cutting line across the circle for the two base panels 4cm from the centre. To make the side panel, join the patches into three rows, each 180cm long. Pin the side edges and machine stitch with a 15mm seam. Press the seam allowance to the right and top stitch 3mm from the seam.

2 With right sides facing, pin the bottom edge of the first strip and the top edge of the second strip together. Machine stitch, again with a 15mm allowance. Join the third strip and press the seam allowances upwards. Top stitch as before.

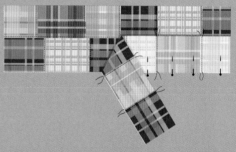

3 Make a similar patchwork panel for the top, from six 75cm rows. Pin on the circle template, centering it. Cut out carefully.

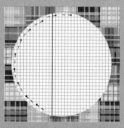

4 Join the short edges of the side panel to make a cylinder, and top stitch the seam.

5 Position eight pins around the top edge of the cylinder at intervals of approximately 22cm. Insert eight pins in the outside edge of the circle, 24cm apart.

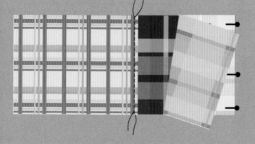

top tip YOU COULD USE THIS ONE-OFF PLAID TO REVAMP AN OLD POUFFE OR OTTOMAN... BUT JUST THINK HOW WONDERFUL A PATCHWORK UPHOLSTERED ARMCHAIR – OR EVEN A SOFA – WOULD LOOK.

Tartan Beanbag

6 With right sides facing, pin the top to the sides, matching up the marker pins first so that they fit together without distortion. Machine stitch all the way round the top, 15mm from the edge.

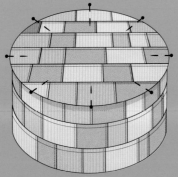

7 Press under a 2cm turning along the straight edge of one base panel. Pull apart the two parts of the velcro. Pin the hooked part across the raw edge, 5mm from the fold and with an equal space at each end. Machine stitch around all four sides, 3mm from the edge.

8 Press a 2cm turning back to the right side of the second base panel and sew the other part of the velcro to it in the same way.

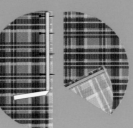

9 Join the two halves of the base by pressing the velcro strips together, but at the same time, slip a sheet of paper between the two parts at the centre so that you can easily separate them later. Pin the slip of paper to the fabric. Top stitch the pieces together at each end between the raw outer edge and the velcro.

10 Pin and stitch the base to the cylinder as for the top in steps 5 and 6.

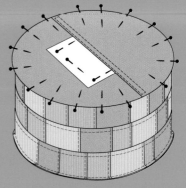

11 Unpin the slip of paper and open out the velcro. Turn right side out and wrestle with the filler until it is inside the cover. You may need to remove some of the beads to make the finished footstool a bit squashier. Close the velcro.

top tip DON'T WORRY TOO MUCH ABOUT THE ORDER IN WHICH YOU ASSEMBLE THE STRIPS – THE COMPLETELY RANDOM ARRANGEMENT OF THE PATTERNS GIVES THIS TYPE OF PATCHWORK ITS INDIVIDUALITY.

Appliqué
Tea Towel

MATERIALS

• patterned fabric • plain tea towel • 15cm spotty ribbon • fusible bonding web • stranded cotton embroidery thread • sewing thread to match ribbon • sewing kit • iron

Appliqué is a great way to repurpose some of the odd remnants that textile magpies just can't help hoarding, just like this length of fifties kitchen fabric with nostalgic imagery. I found the perfect background in a wide linen tea towel with a striped border... but somehow I feel that it might now be more for show than for everyday use.

1 Pick your favourite prints from the appliqué fabric and cut them out roughly. Following the manufacturer's instructions, fuse them to the adhesive side of the bonding web. Use a sheet of paper towel to protect the iron.

2 Cut each motif out with a curved line, following the contour of the image and leaving a 6–10mm margin of plain fabric all round. Peel off the backing papers.

3 Lay the motifs on the tea towel, starting with the largest shapes and filling in the gaps with the smaller ones. Using a hot dry iron, press into position.

4 Edge each motif with a round of blanket stitch, worked with 3 strands of embroidery thread in a matching background colour.

5 Make the ribbon into a hanging loop by folding it in half, turning under the ends and stitching it to the top left corner of the tea towel.

top tip THE BLANKET STITCH EDGING GIVES THESE APPLIQUÉ PATCHES A WONDERFUL FINISH, BUT IF TIME AND PATIENCE ARE LIMITED, SIMPLY ANCHOR THEM DOWN WITH A MACHINED ZIGZAG IN CREAM SEWING THREAD.

Hexagon
Pincushion

MATERIALS

• minimum of 15 x 50cm floral cotton fabric • 10 x 20cm pink cotton fabric • matching sewing thread
• polyester wadding • sewing kit • thick paper for templates

This simple pincushion design, made up of two hexagon rosettes, has been a starter project for generations of hand stitchers. I have given it a twist by making the floral patches identical, so that a new pattern is created when joined together. Known to quilt makers as 'fussy cutting', this is a technique that opens up a whole new way of working with fabric and has endless possibilities. Start by making a different design for the front and back and you'll see what I mean!

1 Cut out 14 paper hexagons for the lining papers following the inner outline template. You'll also need to make a window template to help you choose the best floral motifs and to cut accurate matching patches. Trace both, then cut around to make a hexagonal frame.

2 Pick out your favourite self-contained flower motif and place the window template over it. Draw around the outside of the window, then cut out the hexagon.

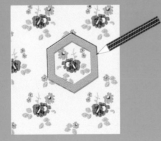

3 Now cut out eleven more matching floral patches. The easiest way to do this is to pin the original patch precisely over a similar motif then cut around the outside edge.

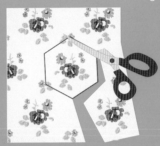

4 Following the outside edge of the window, cut two large pink hexagons for the centre of the rosettes. Pin a template to the centre of a pink hexagon. Working with the template towards you, fold the surplus fabric along one edge forwards and tack it to the paper. Fold the other edges in turn, stitching each one down as you go.

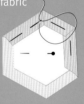

5 Cover all the templates in this way then lay them out in the finished order, checking that the flowers within each rosette all face in the same direction.

top tip 'FUSSY CUTTING' IS A FASCINATING METHOD, BUT IT CAN TAKE UP A LOT OF FABRIC. CHECK THAT YOU HAVE ENOUGH TO MAKE SIX MATCHING HEXAGONS BEFORE YOU START TO CUT OUT THE PATCHES.

Hexagon Pincushion

6 Start by joining the centre to the bottom floral hexagon. Hold the two together with right sides facing, and double check that the innermost edge of the hexagon is at the top. Oversew this edge to the pink hexagon with small stitches, catching a few threads of the fold on each side with each stitch.

7 The next hexagon to the right fits into the angle between these two patches. Check that it is in the right position, then it to the first floral hexagon. Fold in half and sew the next edge to the pink centre. Sew on the other four floral patches in the same way, then make up the second rosette.

8 Pin the two completed rosettes together with the papers facing inwards and over stitch them together around the outside edge. Leave five hexagon sides unstitched at the bottom edge. Press these edges lightly to set the folds. Unpick all the tacking threads and then remove all the paper templates — this will involve a bit of fiddling about I'm afraid!

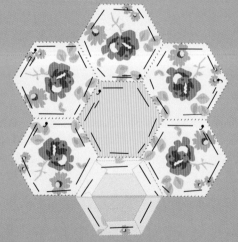

9 Stuff the cushion firmly with polyester filling using a pencil, making sure it reaches right into the corners of the hexagons for a pleasingly plump appearance. Pin the opening and sew four of the edges together. Fill, then slip stitch the final gap.

---

top tip HONEYCOMB PATCHWORK – A PATTERN MADE UP OF MANY INTERLOCKING HEXAGONS – HAS LONG BEEN A FAVOURITE TECHNIQUE FOR MAKING QUILTS, SO PERHAPS THIS PROJECT WILL INSPIRE YOU TO KEEP ON STITCHING.

Personalised Dog Bed

MATERIALS

• lightweight wool blanket • scraps of suede or felt in fawn, red and brown • red embroidery thread • 90 x 60cm canvas • 50cm heavy duty zip • matching sewing thread • sewing machine • sewing kit • 81 x 56 x 15cm dog bed cushion pad (http://www.onlineforpets.co.uk/water-resistant-rectangular-dog-cushion-navy-nylon.html)

CUTTING OUT

from blanket fabric • (A) seventeen 18cm squares • (B) three 14 x 18cm rectangles • (C) three 7 x 18cm rectangles – A, B & C in matching broad stripes • (D) twenty 13 x 18cm rectangles with a narrow stripe pattern
from canvas fabric • one 20 x 55cm rectangle • one 63 x 55cm rectangle

None of my sewing books would be complete without a starring role for Stanley, my beloved Lakeland terrier. So far he has appeared in the guise of a hot water bottle cover, a beanbag and a needlepoint badge, and this time there's even a cuddly toy version of him. This, however, is the one project that I know he'll really enjoy – a warm, woolly patchwork pet bed!

1 Lay out the five rows of patches, following the diagram. The top row starts with a B patch, then has four D patches alternating with three A squares and ends with a narrow C patch. The next row has four D patches alternating with four A squares. These rows are repeated once, then the first row again.

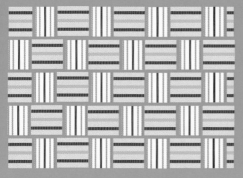

2 Join the patches in each horizontal row with a 1.5cm seam. Press all the seam allowances towards the D patches, then top stitch each seam to strengthen.

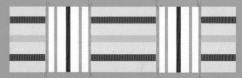

3 Seam the rows together, again with a 1.5cm allowance. Press each allowance downwards and top stitch. Trim a 1.5cm strip from one long edge so the piece measures 103cm by 76.5cm.

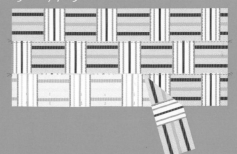

top tip START BY GENTLY LAUNDERING THE BLANKET AND BACKING CANVAS, SO THAT IF YOU EVER NEED TO WASH THE COVER IT WON'T SHRINK ANY FURTHER.

Personalised Dog Bed

4 The corners are stitched at right angles to give depth to the bed. At each corner in turn, fold and pin the two edges together to make a 45 degree angle. Mark a vertical line 12cm in from the corner. Starting 1.5cm up from the bottom edge, stitch along the marked line and trim away the excess fabric, 1cm from the seam.

5 Using the template, cut out a Stanley body from fawn felt or suede, his ear and eye from dark brown and the collar from red. Pin the body to one bottom corner of the dog bed, 15cm in from the edges, and sew him securely in place with small overcast stitches. Add the collar, eye and ear. Write your initials – or your dog's name – in the space above and stitch over the letters in chain stitch, using all six strands of the thread.

6 Press back a 1cm turning along one 55cm edge of each piece of canvas. Tack these folded edges to either side of the zip, leaving a 2.5cm gap at each end and 1cm between the folded edges. Fit a zip foot to your sewing machine and stitch the canvas to the tape, 5mm from the teeth. Tack together the bottom ends of the zip, then open it up.

7 Right sides facing, pin the patchwork to the base, opening out the unstitched seam allowance at the corners. The woollen fabric has more 'give' than the canvas, so you will have to ease the edges of the patchwork to fit the base exactly. Machine stitch twice around the outside edge with a 1.5cm seam.

8 Turn right side out, insert the filler pad and do up the zip. The filler is larger than the cover, to give the finished dog bed a well-stuffed, upholstered look.

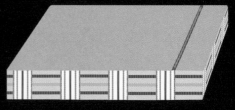

top tip I USED A READY-MADE DOG BED FILLER FROM A SPECIALIST PET SUPPLIER TO GO INSIDE MY COVER, WHICH I CAN EASILY REPLACE WHEN IT BEGINS TO SHOW SIGNS OF WEAR.

Flower Picture

One of the things that I like best about patchwork and appliqué is fact that you will eventually find the perfect use for every single scrap of fabric... even the very smallest fragments! If you are a hoarder (like me), you're bound to have a stash of offcuts, buttons, threads, beads and ribbons that have been left over from other projects, and this spectacular flower picture is a fantastic way to get creative with them.

1 Start by making the crazy patchwork vase. Make a paper template and pin it centrally to the white fabric. Draw round the outside edge and unpin. Fill in the shape with scraps of dress weight prints and shirting, arranging them so the background is covered completely and the fabric overlaps the outline by 2cm all round. Pin as you go.

2 Work a row of decorative embroidery over every join, using three strands of cream thread. I chose fly stitch as an alternative to the feather stitch on the Crazy Patch Cushion. You can see how to work both of these on page 29, along with the other stitches I used here: straight stitch, chain stitch and single feather stitch.

3 Using the template as your guide, cut a vase from batting. Pin this centrally to the back of the completed patchwork vase and trim the margin to 1mm all round. Snip into the curves, then turn back the margin around the top and side edges and tack it down.

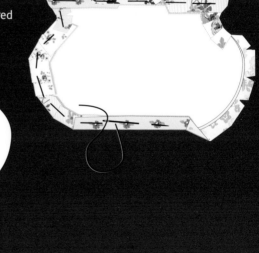

MATERIALS

• large white damask napkin • striped tea towel • 35 x 25cm plain white cotton • 30 x 20cm quilt batting
• scraps of floral, check and striped print fabric • floral furnishing fabric • plain green cotton fabric • fusible
bonding web • buttons • stranded cotton embroidery thread in shades of green, red and cream • sewing kit
• sewing machine

4 Pin the vase centrally along one long edge of the napkin, 15mm from the edge, and slip stitch it in place. Cut a 15cm strip from one long edge of the striped towel, the same length as the napkin. With right sides facing, pin it along the edge of the napkin and over the bottom of the vase. Sew the two together with a 15mm seam, then press the seam towards the stripes.

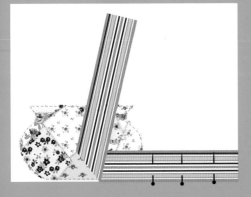

5 Select the prettiest flowers from the furnishing fabric and cut them out roughly. Following the manufacturer's instructions, iron the wrong side onto the bonding web and then cut out neatly around the outside edge of each motif.

6 Draw a few simple leaf shapes on to the paper side of the bonding web and fuse it to the back of the green fabric. Cut them out around the pencil lines. Make four or more Suffolk puffs, as shown on page 147 and using the bonding web, cut circles of fabric to go behind them.

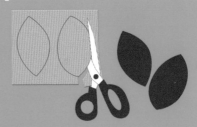

top tip NO TWO APPLIQUÉ PICTURES WILL EVER BE THE SAME, SO USE MY DESIGN AS A SPRINGBOARD FOR YOUR OWN IDEAS.

SEARCH THROUGH YOUR TEXTILE COLLECTION AND TAKE INSPIRATION FROM THE FABRICS YOU FIND THERE.

Flower
Picture

7 Now it's time for some flower arranging. Starting with the largest blooms, position the flowers, leaves, circles and puffs around the vase and shuffle them about until you're pleased with the design. Draw in the curving stems with a dressmaker's pen or chalk pencil, then remove the vase.

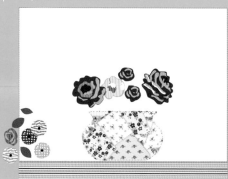

8 Peel off the backing papers and press down the flowers, circles and leaves. Slip stitch around the edge of the puffs.

9 Embroider over the stalk lines in green chain stitch and around the edge of the flowers using a variety of stitches to give texture to your picture.

10 Sew the matching buttons in groups of three to fill the spaces between the motifs and add others to the flower centres.

top tip TAKE THIS DESIGN FURTHER BY COMBINING IT WITH MACHINE PATCHWORK. YOU COULD ADD A DEEP BORDER OF PATCHWORK SQUARES AND USE THE FLOWER BOWL AS THE CENTREPIECE FOR A SMALL QUILT.

Bunny Sweater

MATERIALS

• floral print fabric • 10cm of 2cm wide ribbon • black and red stranded cotton embroidery thread • fusible bonding web • pencil • sewing kit

Hand knitted garments have a charm all of their own and are so much more appealing than machine made versions. I couldn't resist adding a flowered appliqué rabbit to this tiny V-necked sweater, along with a matching update of the classic elbow patch. The patches are purely decorative, but you could copy the idea if you ever need to cover up any moth holes or areas where the yarn has worn thin.

1 Trace the reversed rabbit template and two circles on to the paper side of the bondaweb, fuse to the wrong side of the fabric and cut out around the outlines. Peel off the backing papers.

2 Position the rabbit centrally on the front of the sweater. Using a cloth to protect the wool from the heat, press it in place with a warm iron. Fuse the circles to the back of the sleeves.

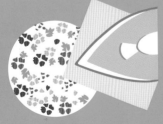

3 Working with three strands of red thread, embroider a round of tailor's buttonhole stitch (see page 29) around the edge of each patch. Sew the bunny's eye in black satin stitch, then add three short straight stitches for the whiskers and a satin stitch nose.

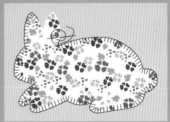

4 To make the bow, cut a 7cm length from the ribbon. Fold it into a loop with the ends at the back. Stitching through all three layers, gather the centre of the ribbon. Fold the remaining piece in half widthways and wrap around the gathered part. Sew the ends securely to the wrong side, then sew the bow to the bunny.

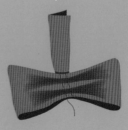

top tip IF YOU PREFER TO USE TRADITIONAL SOFT LEATHER OR SUEDE FOR THE ELBOW PATCHES, YOU WILL NEED TO STITCH WITH A SPECIAL TRIANGULAR NEEDLE. THIS PIERCES THE LEATHER WITHOUT CAUSING IT TO SPLIT.

Patched Dungarees

MATERIALS

• torn garment • scraps of cotton duck or denim • scraps of spot print cotton • small piece of quilt wadding • matching sewing thread • sewing machine

Here is another example of functional patching, this time on the knees of a pair of toddler-sized dungarees. Once small children start crawling about it's always the knee areas that seem to get the most wear and tear, so these padded racing car patches will cover up the damage as well as providing extra protection. I added the two spot print patches – cut from old handkerchiefs – for a bit of extra pattern and colour.

1 Start by repairing the tear or hole. Undo the poppers at the inside legs and work several closely spaced lines of machine stitch to and fro across the gap. Use the reverse lever to stitch backwards.

2 Cut two 8cm squares from the spotty fabrics and press under a 5mm turning around each edge of them both. Cut two 11cm squares from the heavier fabric: make them larger if you have a big rip to conceal. From the wadding cut two 10cm squares.

3 The large patches go centrally over the darns and the spotty squares peep out from behind them. Work out the positions, then machine stitch the spotty patches in place with a narrow zigzag in matching thread.

4 Place the wadding in position, then pin the large patches down over them. Rethread the sewing machine with a colour to match, then zigzag down.

top tip WHEN YOU ARE MAKING A REPAIR PATCH, MAKE SURE THAT IT IS A SIMILAR WEIGHT TO THE GARMENT. I USED COTTON DUCK ON THESE CANVAS DUNGAREES, BUT DENIM WOULD HAVE WORKED JUST AS WELL.

Puff Collar Cardigan

MATERIALS

• cardigan • selection of print fabrics – about 12cm square for each puff • pair of compasses and paper
• self-cover buttons • matching sewing thread • sewing kit

When I was planning the square cushion cover on page 90, all of the Suffolk Puffs were randomly strewn across my desk. I loved the mixture of fabrics, so started wondering whether there was another way in which I could use these pretty little patches. I came up with the idea of embellishing a cashmere cardigan with a 'collar' of puffs... great to wear over a summery floral dress.

1 Cut an 11cm diameter disc of paper. Using this as a template, cut about 35 circles from the various fabrics and make them up into Suffolk Puffs, as shown on page 91.

2 Pin a row of puffs all the way around the neckline, at front and back, then arrange the rest on the front to create a symmetrical collar shape. Overlap the edges of a few and pin in place. Depending on the size and shape of your cardigan, you may need to make a few more puffs to fill all the spaces.

3 Sew each puff down with a round of small straight stitches in matching thread. You'll need to stitch through all the layers where the puffs overlap.

4 It's the details that make things really special, so as a finishing touch I replaced the basic buttons on this cardigan with small, round self-cover buttons, made from the floral fabric offcuts. The button kits provide all the instructions for how to do this.

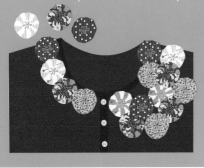

top tip CHOOSE A NARROW COLOUR PALETTE TO COMPLEMENT YOUR CARDIGAN. I USED STRIPES, SPOTS AND GINGHAM IN SHADES OF PINK AND RED, THEN ADDED A SPRINKLING OF PUFFS IN A CO-ORDINATING FLOWERED DRESS FABRIC.

Puff
Necklace

MATERIALS
• scraps of plain and floral print dress-weight fabric • matching sewing thread • one long or two short chain necklaces • masking tape • sewing kit

CUTTING OUT
from floral print fabric • one 12cm circle • two 10cm circles • two 8cm circles
from plain fabric • two 12cm circles • two 8cm circles

Last but not least, is this sweet puff necklace – the ideal accessory to wear with your favourite floaty summer frock, or even over a plain sweater. Offcuts of viscose crepe were used, which gives the puffs an especially three-dimensional aspect, but it would look just as good in any floral print with a toning plain fabric.

1 Make all the circles of fabric into puffs, as for the cushion cover on page 91. Lay them out in decreasing size to form a horseshoe shape, with the largest puff at the centre.

2 Pin the puffs to each other where they overlap, keeping them in the same formation. Sew them together with small stab stitches, sewing through all the layers of fabric.

3 Turn the puffs over and place the chain centrally across the back, following the curve. Secure it in place with short lengths of masking tape, then sew the chain to the back of the puffs.

top tip INSTEAD OF SEWING THE PUFFS TO A CHAIN, YOU COULD STITCH A LENGTH OF NARROW RIBBON TO EACH END:
3MM-WIDE SATIN RIBBON WOULD BE SUITABLY DELICATE, OR TRY A WIDER DOUBLE-FACED VELVET FOR A LUXE LOOK.

Useful Addresses

Patchwork shops

The Bramble Patch
West Street
Weedon
Northamptonshire NN7 4QU
01327 342121
www.thebramblepatch.co.uk

Coast & Country Crafts & Quilts
Barras Moor Farm
Perranarworthal, Truro
Cornwall TR3 7PE
01872 870478
www.coastandcountrycrafts.co.uk

The Cotton Patch
1285 Stratford Road
Hall Green
Birmingham B28 9AJ
0121 7022840
www.cottonpatch.net

Creative Quilting
32 Bridge Road
Hampton Court Village
East Molesey
Surrey KT8 9HA
020 8941 7075
www.creativequilting.co.uk

The Fat Quarters
5 Chopwell Road
Blackhall Mill
Newcastle Upon Tyne NE17 7TN
01207 565728
www.thefatquarters.co.uk

Heirs & Graces
Wesleyan House
Dale Road
Darley Dale
Derbyshire DE4 2HX
01629 734100
www.patchworkdirect.com

Patch – Fabric and Haberdashery
9 Bevan Street East
Lowestoft
Suffolk NR32 2AA
01502 588778
www.patchfabrics.co.uk

Patchwork Garden
630 Abbeydale Road
Sheffield
South Yorkshire S7 2BA
0114 258 3763
www.patchworkgarden.co.uk

Pelenna Patchworks
5 Bevans Terrace
Pontrhydyfen
Port Talbot
West Glamorgan SA12 9TR
01639 898444
www.pelennapatchworks.co.uk

Quilter's Haven
68 High Street
Wickham Market
Woodbridge
Suffolk IP13 0QU
01728 746275
www.quilters-haven.co.uk

Tikki
293 Sandycombe Road
Kew
Surrey TW9 3LU
020 8948 8462
www.tikkilondon.com

Fabric and haberdashery shops

Bedecked
5 Castle Street
Hay-on-Wye
Hereford HR3 5DF
01497 822769
www.bedecked.co.uk

Cloth House
47 Berwick Street
London W1F 8SJ
020 7437 5155
www.clothhouse.net

Design-a-Cushions
74 Drum Brae South
Edinburgh EH12 8TH
0131 539 0080
www.deisgn-a-cushions.co.uk

Harts of Hertford
14 Bull Plain
Hertford SG14 1DT
01992 558106
www.hartsofhertford.com

John Lewis
Oxford Street
London W1A 1EX
and branches nationwide
08456 049049
www.johnlewis.com

MacCulloch & Wallis
25–26 Dering Street
London W1S 1AT
020 7629 0311
www.macculloch-wallis.co.uk

The Makery Emporium
16 Northumberland Place
Bath
Avon BA1 5AR
01225 487708
www.themakeryonline.co.uk

Mandors
134 Renfrew Street
Glasgow G3 6ST
0141 332 7716
www.mandors.co.uk

Merrick & Day
Redbourne Road
Redbourne
Gainsborough
Lincolnshire DN21 4TG
01652 648 814
www.merrick-day.com

Millie Moon
20 Paul Street
Frome
Somerset BA11 1DT
01373 464650
www.milliemoonshop.co.uk

Our Patterned Hand
49 Broadway Market
London E8 4PH
020 7812 9912
www.ourpatternedhand.co.uk

Rags
19 Chapel Walk
Crowngate Shopping Centre
Worcester WR1 3LD
01905 612330

Sew and So's
14 Upper Olland Street
Bungay
Suffolk NR35 1BG
01986 896147
www.sewandsos.co.uk

Patchwork and sewing classes

Heatherlea Design
01332 661562
www.heatherleadesign.com

Just Between Friends
44 Station Way
Buckhurst Hill
Essex IG9 6LN
020 8502 9191
www.justbetweenfriends.co.uk

Liberty Sewing School
Regent Street
London W1B 5AH
www.liberty.co.uk

The Makery
146 Walcot Street
Bath
Avon BA1 5BL
01225 421175
www.themakeryonline.co.uk

Sew Over It
78 Landor Road
Clapham North
London SW9 9PH
020 7326 0376
www.sewoverit.co.uk

The Thrifty Stitcher
Unit 21
4–6 Shelford Place
Stoke Newington
London N16 9HS
07779 255087
www.thethriftystitcher.co.uk

Modern Approach Sewing School
Astra Business Centre
Roman Way
Ribbleton
Preston PR2 5AP
01772 498862
www.sewjanetmoville.co.uk

Sue Hazell Sewing Tuition
Southcombe House
Chipping Norton
Oxfordshire OX7 5QH
www.sewing-tuition.co.uk

The Studio London
Studio 5
Trinity Buoy Wharf
64 Orchard Place
London E14 0JW
www.thestudiolondon.co.uk

Cath Kidston Stores

Aberdeen
Unit GS20, Union Square Centre
Aberdeen AB11 5PN
01224 591 726

Bath
3 Broad Street, Milsom Place
Bath BA1 5LJ
01225 331 006

Belfast
24–26 Arthur Street
Belfast BT1 4GF
02890 231 581

Bluewater
Unit L003 Rose Gallery
Bluewater Centre DA9 9SH
01322 387 454

Bournemouth
5–6 The Arcade
Old Christchurch Road
Bournemouth BH1 2AF
01202 553 848

Brighton
31a & 32 East Street
Brighton BN1 1HL
01273 227 420

Bristol
79 Park Street
Bristol BS1 5PF
0117 930 4722

Cambridge
31–33 Market Hill
Cambridge CB2 3NU
01223 351 810

Canterbury
6 The Parade
Canterbury CT1 2JL
01227 455 639

Cardiff
45 The Hayes
Cardiff CF10 1GA
02920 225 627

Cheltenham
21 The Promenade
Cheltenham GL50 1LE
01242 245 912

Chester
12 Eastgate Streets
Chester CH1 1LE
01244 310 685

Chichester
24 South Street
Chichester PO19 1EL
01243 850 100

Dublin
Unit CSD 1.3, Dundrum Centre
Dublin 16
01 296 4430

Edinburgh
58 George Street
Edinburgh EH2 2LR
0131 220 1509

Exeter
6 Princesshay
Exeter EX1 1GE
01392 227 835

Glasgow
18 Gordon Street
Glasgow G1 3PB
0141 248 2773

Guildford
14–18 Chertsey Street
Guildford GU1 4HD
01483 564 798

Harrogate
2–6 James Street
Harrogate HG1 1RF
01423 531 481

Jersey
11 King Street
St Helier JE2 4WF
01534 726 768

Kildare
Unit 21c Kildare Village
Nurney Road, Kildare Town
00 353 45 535 084

Kingston
10 Thames Street
Kingston Upon Thames KT1 1PE
020 8546 6760

Leeds
26 Lands Lane
Leeds LS1 6LB
0113 391 2692

Liverpool
18 School Lane
Liverpool L1 3BT
0151 709 2747

London – Battersea
142 Northcote Road
London SW11 6RD
020 7228 6571

London – Chiswick
125 Chiswick High Road
London W4 2ED
020 8995 8052

London – Covent Garden
28–32 Shelton Street
London WC2H 9JE
020 7836 4803

London – Fulham
668 Fulham Road
London SW6 5RX
020 7731 6531

London – Heathrow Terminal 4
Heathrow Airport TW6 3XA
020 8759 5578

London – Kings Road
322 Kings Road
London SW3 5UH
020 7351 7335

London – Marylebone
51 Marylebone High Street
London W1U 5HW
020 7935 6555

London – Notting Hill
158 Portobello Road
London W11 2BE
020 7727 0043

London – Sloane Square
27 Kings Road
London SW3 4RP
020 7259 9847

London – St Pancras
St Pancras International Station
London NW1 2QP
020 7837 4125

London – Wimbledon Village
3 High Street
Wimbledon SW19 5DX
020 8944 1001

Manchester
62 King Street
Manchester M2 4ND
0161 8347 936

Marlborough
142–142a High Street
Marlborough SN8 1HN
01672 512 514

Newbury
Unit G42 Middle Street, Parkway
Newbury RG14 1AY

Newcastle
136–138 Grainger Street
Newcastle NE1 5AF

Norwich
21 Castle Street
Norwich NR2 1PB

Nottingham
23 Bridesmith Gate
Nottingham NG1 2GR

Oxford
6 Broad Street
Oxford OX1 3AJ
01865 791 576

Reading
96 Broad Street
Reading RG1 2AP
01189 588 530

St Albans
Unit 4 Christopher Place
St Albans AL3 5DQ
01727 810 432

St Ives
67 Fore Street
St Ives TR26 1HE
01736 798 001

Sheffield
60 High Street
Meadowhall
Sheffield S9 1EN

Tunbridge Wells
59–61 High Street
Tunbridge Wells TN1 1XU
01892 521 197

Winchester
46 High Street
Winchester SO23 9BT
01962 870 620

Windsor
24 High Street
Windsor SL4 1LH
01753 830 591

York
32 Stonegate
York YO1 8AS
01904 733 653

Concessions in:
Bicester Village, OX26 6WD
Gunwharf Quays, PO1 3TU
Fenwicks, Northumberland Street,
  Newcastle Upon Tyne NE99 1AR
Selfridges, The Bull Ring, Birmingham
  B5 4BP
Selfridges, Oxford Street, London
  W1A 1AB
Selfridges, Exchange Square,
  Manchester M3 1BD
Selfridges, Trafford Centre,
  Manchester M17 8DA

For up-to-date information on all
Cath Kidston stores, please visit
www.cathkidston.com.

Acknowledgements

My special thanks to everyone involved in the creation of this book: to Elaine Ashton and Jessica Pemberton, to Lucinda Ganderton and her assistant Lis Gunner for the making of the projects, to Pia Tryde for her inspiring photography, and to Anne Furniss, Helen Lewis, Lisa Pendreigh and Katherine Case at Quadrille.

Cath Kidston

Series Creative Coordinator: Elaine Ashton
Design Assistant to Cath Kidston: Jessica Pemberton
Patchwork Coordinator and Consultant: Lucinda Ganderton
Patchwork Assistant: Lis Gunner

Editorial Director: Anne Furniss
Art Director: Helen Lewis
Project Editor: Lisa Pendreigh
Designer: Katherine Case
Photographer: Pia Tryde
Illustrators: Bridget Bodoano and Joy FitzSimmons
Pattern Checker: Sally Harding
Production Director: Vincent Smith
Production Controller: Aysun Hughes

Quadrille *craft*

www.quadrillecraft.co.uk

If you have any comments or queries regarding the instructions in this book, please contact us at enquiries@quadrille.co.uk.

This edition first published in 2013 by
Quadrille Publishing Limited
Alhambra House
27–31 Charing Cross Road
London WC2H 0LS

Text copyright © Cath Kidston 2011
Design templates and projects © Cath Kidston 2011
Photography © Pia Tryde 2011
Design and layout copyright © Quadrille Publishing Limited 2011

Cataloguing-in-Publication Data: a catalogue record for this book is available from the British Library.

ISBN 978 184949 264 5